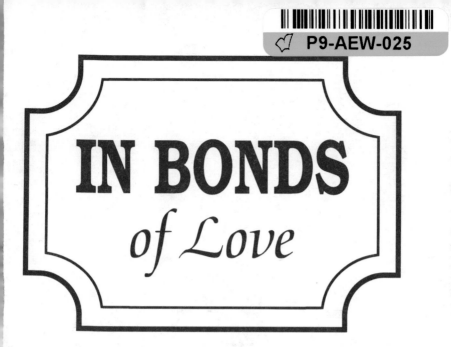

IN BONDS
of Love

by
Nathaniel J. Wilson

Reach Worldwide, Inc.
P.O. Box 292100
Sacramento, CA 95829

In Bonds of Love

Printed in the United States of America

Cover Design by Nathaniel J. Wilson and Matt Jones
Cover Illustration by Matt Jones

About the Cover

There is an ear on the front cover. It has been pierced through and is bleeding. Some are puzzled when they first notice it. I hope you understand it more clearly when you have finished the book.

Dedicated
to

Doug		Myles
&	and	&
Rebecca		Sheila

and to precious
sons and daughters
everywhere who have
the scarred ear.

Special Thanks

To me, knowing Jesus Christ is the most unspeakably exciting thing in all of human experience. If you believe He created worlds, and that the universe is "held together" by Him (I do so believe! Col. 1:15-17), then to know Him intimately as your personal Lord and friend is the most fantastic thing indeed. I do know Him as such, and have for over thirty-five years. He has been (and is) nothing short of spectacular. He is "the way" which has shown us "the way". To Him I am thankful.

Further, to live with someone who epitomizes His Spirit and teachings is an additional blessing. Mary Wilson is such a person. Loving, loyal, dedicated, full of laughter. Yet, deeply spiritual, with a strength of character that I have peered down into for years, and never found the bottom. A vivacious, christian leader of powerful, vivacious, christian women. She is my best friend. I thank God for my great wife.

To produce this book within the time-frame allotted us would have been impossible without the very able assistance of my secretary, Susan Pope, and Peggy Pope, her mother. Much credit is due their dedication and commitment, coupled with their enormous capacity for getting things done quickly and efficiently. I could not have done it without them (and Jerry, who was willing to put up with their nocturnal ways).

Thank you, Sheila, for inspiring me with your interest in things biblical.

Thank you, Rebecca, for helping with research after graduation from college.

Thank you to a great people, The Rock Church, for letting me be your pastor. You have taught me much.

Table of Contents

Introduction

As a reader of this opening introductory line, it follows that you might decide to read the rest of this little book. In case this should happen, I want to take this opportunity to say "welcome". Certainly there would be little use for a book if there was no one interested in reading it.

However, most books are written to fill a perceived need. Therefore, most books have a particular audience or group in mind when they are written. Others may read it and find it useful. If that happens, the author is happy. However, that is counted as an additional, positive result that is like "icing on the cake".

Although anyone is welcome to read the following pages, this book, like most others, is not written for everyone. It is written with a particular audience in mind. It addresses things that would be of little interest to many, but very important to its particular audience.

To prevent misunderstanding, it should be clarified that its aim at an intended audience is not because that audience is assumed to be better or worse than others, nor because of any supposed intellectual or moral superiority of its intended readership. Neither does the fact that it is not intended for everyone mean that it is something mysterious, for it is not that either. In addition, neither is its purpose to convince those which would disagree with its conclusions.

So, although none of the above are the reasons for it being written, there is nevertheless an important reason, and it is addressed to a specific group. The group being addressed can be found by taking a look at an ancient biblical custom given in the Old Testament.

Chapter 1

An Ancient Biblical Custom

It was no different in ancient days than it is today. Then, as now, society had the poor among them. As a class, "the poor" are spoken of often in scripture. Even a casual Bible reader will recognize that God always made provision for the poor, especially those who were so hopeless they simply could not help themselves. The whole Bible, particularly the New Testament, equates the idea of the well-off helping the hopelessly poor as a parallel to God giving His riches and glory to us - the spiritually poor who are without help and without hope (Eph. 1:7,8, 2:4-6; Lk. 4:18; Rom. 5:6-8, etc.).

In the Old Testament, a citizen could become so poor that he or she could lose everything they had. This could happen through no fault of his own, or could happen through mismanagement of one's

3

resources. Regardless of the reason for it happening, if he lost all, the last resort was that, if he had nothing else to use as payment to his creditor, the creditor could claim him as a slave to defray the amount of his overwhelming debt. When he had nothing else to offer, he was required to offer himself - thus becoming a slave (or servant). Because of the weight of his debt, servitude was the only hope of ever escaping his crushing burden. His creditor became his master.

This, of course, is likened to Christ's gift of salvation to the New Testament believer. We were alienated, "broke", poor, without recourse, and hopelessly in debt (Rom. 3:10-19). The only way to satisfy our debt was to become His servant. We belong to Him. He is our Master. We became His property. In return, we have been taken into His house of plenty. His supply becomes ours. He gives us His protection. We lost our freedom, but we did gain His provision - and in due process came to know our Master intimately.

However, a day came when the servant could go free. After six years of servitude (on the seventh year), the Bible declared the master was to give the indebted slave the option of leaving. He did not have to stay (Ex. 21:2). In fact, even if he chose to leave, the master would bless him as he left. Even though he was no longer in that household, he went out blessed for having been there. Though he came as a debtor, and even after six years still owed much, nevertheless on the seventh year (when he chose to go), the master blessed him. Not that it was merited.

4

love my master, my wife, and my children; I will not go out free" (Ex. 21:5).

When this happened, he was then brought by his master unto the judges to witness that he had chosen the master's house. He was taken to the door (or lintel) of the house, and an awl was used to bore a mark through his ear which marked him forever. This was a symbol that he was fastened to the master's house forever. Once this was done, the declaration was made of a new covenant relationship between the servant and his master.

"...he shall serve him forever" (Ex. 21:6).

This new covenant relationship was grounded in love alone. The master's wishes became the servant's commands. The master's ways, judgments, instructions, and guidelines, became the servant's way of life forever. It was an unshakable bond, grounded in an unshakable relationship. The servant and the master were beyond being simply bound legally. This was no legalism. This bondage was one of deep and abiding commitment, wherein one only sought what pleases the other. Self-will was swallowed up in sacrificial love. Thus, the servant was forever willingly captured in bonds of love.

That brings us to the purpose of this book. Again, we are happy if you enjoy it regardless of who you are. However, the purpose of this book is to edify those servants of Christ who are happily captured and held to Him...

"IN BONDS OF LOVE"

Chapter 2

Terms Of Relationship

As we have already seen in the Old Testament example of the love-slave, scripture uses numerous relational examples to illustrate our relationship to Christ. Other Old Testament examples (besides the love-slave) are the kinsman-redeemer, the eagle and her young, a wise/benevolent king and His subjects, a covenant relationship between God and His people, etc. All of these are reinforcements to the idea of a love relationship, with the lesser receiving benefits by following the loving guidance and enlightenment from the greater.

The New Testament expands this idea dramatically. We are not only the Lord's servants, but also His children (Jn. 1:12,13). As such, we are bound to Him - not by fear, but by love (Rom. 8:15).

Not only are we children, but as such are "heirs of God, and joint-heirs with Christ" (Rom. 8:1-17).

Scripture contains many examples of our relationship with God as being one of love and mutual desire to please. The legal facts of judgment and damnation for disobedience remain real. However, for the child of God who has lived for the Lord faithfully, the bond has long since transcended fear and consciousness of legal obligations, and is likened to the bond between a husband and wife.

> *"Husbands love your wives, even as Christ also loved the church, and gave Himself for it; So ought men to love their wives as their own bodies. He that loveth his wife loveth himself. For we are members of His body, of His flesh and of His bones. This is a great mystery: but I speak concerning Christ and the church"* *(Eph. 5:25,28,32).*

These scriptural parallels are drawn to illustrate Christ's relationship with the church. Each attempts to show the love bond between Christ and individual believers, as well as the church collectively.

In each example, it is made graphically clear that the relationship hinges on the reciprocal faithfulness of the two parties. God provides, protects, nurtures, fulfills, expands, guides, instructs, and leads the believer. The believer, in turn, is faithful to follow, obey, grow, receive instruction, be grateful, and become their best in service to (and relationship with) the Lord. This was all based on an old, old, biblical precept of biblical covenants.

Biblical Covenants

Biblically, there is a great difference between "covenant" people and other people. Covenant people enjoy benefits that non-covenant people do not. For example, when David was confronted with Goliath, he was incredulous that God's army should be dismayed by this "uncircumcised Philistine". Circumcision was a sign (or symbol) of a covenant between God and His people, Israel. When David declared Goliath to be "an uncircumcised Philistine", he was in effect declaring that this man had no real power over God's people because he had no covenant with the God who gives victory. In contrast, David carefully articulates God's oneness with Israel as His covenant people. David depends upon this covenant relationship as the basis for his faith that God will give him/them certain victory - which He does.

Not only did covenants have benefits, but they also had obligations. The tremendous blessing, which God promised in the covenant relationship, was never without reciprocal obligations. People could actually "get away" with things before they were a covenant people that they were held strictly accountable for after becoming a covenant people.

For example, in ancient covenants (religious or secular) murmuring against the covenant giver was always treated as violation of the obligation of the subordinate member of the covenant. These

13

murmurings by Israel in the wilderness were punished (Num. 11). Paul uses these very murmurings to point out that this rule is still intact under the new covenant, or New Testament. (I Cor. 10:1-7). However, when the children of Israel first came out of Egypt, they murmured (Ex. 17:2-7), but were not punished. The difference is that this murmuring was before the establishing of God's covenant with them at Mt. Sinai. From this we see with unmistakable clarity that a covenant people are never "free" in the sense of not being responsible to follow the covenant-givers covenant obligations. When this is contrasted with the modern idea of christian freedom being license to indulge in the conduct, ideas, and actions of non-covenant people, it is readily apparent that such teachings are not only fallacious, but patently dangerous.

The above paragraph is especially true in light of the fact that another obligation of ancient covenants (both biblical and secular) was that the covenant required the exclusion of relationships to other sovereign powers. "First, the vassal must not enter into alliances with other independent kings, and he must be a friend to the suzerain's (king's) friends, and an enemy to his enemies".[1]

From this we see that there was an exclusivity and possessiveness built into the covenant relationship. A certain jealous guarding of the covenant-givers interests and good name was expected. "Obedience to the commands of God took precedence over other concerns...", and there were stipulations "...to which the vassal binds himself in accepting the covenant defined by the suzerain".[2] Being as God's people are a covenant-people, we can see from this that it becomes increasingly important for the servant of the Lord to understand the framework within which our relationship with our Lord is maintained.

Biblical covenants were sealed with an oath. The oath was a promise, solemnly made. This oath was sometimes a spoken formula, and sometimes a formal action or ceremony which "sealed" the covenant. For example, the covenant which God made with Noah (Noahic) was sealed with the rainbow. The covenant with Abraham was sealed with circumcision. The covenant with Moses was sealed with written tablets of stone. As is evident, the sealing of a covenant with an oath could take a wide variety of forms. Whatever the form, the main idea was that it set apart the covenant as being a forever binding agreement between God and His people. Obviously, this was something which was never to be entered into casually or without solemn thought (Lk. 14:28-33). Like most things in the Old Testament, the covenants found there were but partial. Only in the New Testament is the covenant idea completed.

Jesus Himself introduces the "new covenant", upon which the christian's relationship with Christ in His church is based. This new covenant is different and much more powerful than any of the Old Testament covenants. It takes on a cosmic nature as opposed to the land-based covenants before. The church is spoken of as "pilgrims and strangers" in this world, whose inheritance is in the heavenlies.

> "...come unto mount Zion, and unto the city of the living God, the heavenly Jerusalem and to an innumerable company of angels, to the general assembly and church of the firstborn which are written in heaven..." (Heb. 12:22,23).

To introduce this new covenant, Christ declares at the Last Supper: "This is the blood of the new covenant {Gr. diathekes}..." (Mt. 26:28). Here He uses Old Testament language taken from Exodus 24:8.

> "...Behold the blood of the covenant, which the Lord hath made with you..." (Ex. 24:8).

Jesus here presented Himself as a sacrifice, the new Passover Lamb, whose death instituted the new covenant which was foreshadowed in the making of the covenant on Sinai.[3]

The institution of the Lord's Supper is one of several prominent actions (symbolic and otherwise) which are found in the New Testament, and serve as signs and sureties of the new covenant relationship. When we say that God instituted "signs" ("symbols" of His covenants with man), we do not mean that it was simply the outward symbol of some internal happening. In the context of covenants, a "sign" (Gr. semeion) means "a mark" or indication which distinguishes a person or thing from others. In other words, the sign of the covenant sets a man apart as God's personal property".[4]

At other times, this sign was spoken of as a "seal". Paul, in describing circumcision, calls it a "seal of righteousness". Seal (Gr. spragis) denotes an emblem of ownership and security. Specifically, this seal was an impression made by the signet ring of one in authority, such as a king. The word, as it is used in the New Testament, includes the meaning of destination, so that the persons sealed are secured from destruction and marked for reward.[5] An example of this use is found in Paul's letter to Timothy.

> *"Nevertheless the foundation of God standeth sure, having this seal, The Lord knoweth them that are His. And, let everyone that nameth the name of Christ depart from iniquity" (II Tim. 2:19).*

With the beginning of Christ's church in Acts 2, God established a new covenant "sign" or "seal" that signified entrance into the body of God's new covenant people. In the same way that circumcision became the initiating rite into the old covenant, so water and spirit baptism became the initiating rite in the new covenant. The old covenant of Abraham, as well as the covenant with Moses, included the shedding of blood, or a "dying out" to the past. Repentance is the new covenant equivalent of "dying out" to sin and judgment. Water baptism is the New Testament initiation rite into the covenant community which followed repentance, and is shown, along with spirit baptism, to be the New Testament fulfillment of Old Testament circumcision.

> *"In whom also ye are circumcised with the circumcision made without hands, in putting off the body of the sins of the flesh, by the circumcision of Christ; Buried with him in baptism, wherein also ye are risen with him through the faith of the operation of God, who hath raised him from the dead (Col. 2:11).*

Not only was the act of water baptism an initiatory rite into the New Testament covenant community, but it is also significant that it was administered in the name of Jesus (Acts 2:38, 8:16, 10:48, 19:5, etc.). Thus, the sign of the covenant bore the "signature" of the one the baptismal candidate was being buried with in covenant relationship (Rom. 6:4).

Along with water baptism, Spirit baptism is also likened to old covenant circumcision.

> *"For he is not a Jew, which is one outwardly; neither is that circumcision, which is outward in the flesh: But he is a Jew, which is one inwardly; and circumcision is that of the heart, in the spirit, and not in the letter; whose praise is not of men, but of God" (Rom. 2:28,29).*

> *"For we are the circumcision, which worship God in the Spirit, and rejoice in Christ Jesus, and have no confidence in the flesh" (Phil. 3:3).*

As we have already seen, Paul also used the term "seal" to describe the sign of the covenant. This term is also used to describe the new covenant seal as it refers to Spirit baptism.

18

"Who hath also sealed us, and given the earnest of the Spirit in our hearts..." (II Cor. 1:22).

"...ye were sealed with that Holy Spirit of promise" (Eph. 1:13).

"...and grieve not the Holy Spirit of God, whereby ye are sealed unto the day of redemption" (Eph. 4:30).

The fact that the New Testament church was under a new and dynamic covenant relationship is a fact not overlooked by the Old Testament. Jeremiah saw this.

"Behold, the days come, saith the Lord, that I will make a new covenant with the house of Israel, and with the house of Judah: Not according to the covenant that I made with their fathers in the day that I took them by the hand to bring them out of the land of Egypt; which my covenant they brake, although I was an husband unto them, saith the Lord; But this shall be the covenant that I will make with the house of Israel; After those days, saith the Lord, I will put my law in their inward parts, and write in their hearts; and will be their God, and they shall be my people" (Jer. 31:31-33).

Initiation into the new covenant community in Bible days was capsulized in Acts 2:38. The careful student of the Word of God could hardly come to any other conclusion than that the consistent and only door into the New Testament church was: "Repent and be baptized everyone of you in the name of Jesus Christ for the remission of sins, and ye shall receive the gift of the Holy Ghost" (Acts 2:38).

19

In conclusion, it is evident from this brief discussion of covenants that, if one believes the Bible to be God's Word, then it is indeed a sobering thing to be in covenant relationship with God.

It means that one should have a strong, healthy grasp on what the Covenant-God wants and expects from the covenanted believer. One must keep in mind that the freedom entered into as a result of the covenant relationship is akin to a marriage - exhilarating, intensely fulfilling, deeply personal, but always maintained within the stipulations of the agreement. To ignore the guidelines is to destroy the relationship.

I believe it is of great importance that today we understand our covenant relationship with God. Since time immemorial, sober people have thought that there time had become the "worse yet". Because we live in it, our time can seem worse than others. However, in the history of America, I think it goes without saying, there has never been a time when the nation drifted as morally rudderless as it does today. One does not have to be a sociologist to know that moral decline is not only the order of the day, but is actually celebrated as progress. How quickly things change - in Russia the government is sponsoring christian schools, and in America prayer is prohibited in government schools under the guise of "freedom". Someone has rightly said that it cannot be 100 degrees outside and not affect the inside. What is true in the world is paralleled in the church world. Convoluted thinking seems to be prevalent in many quarters. Everything from perversion to agnosticism is deemed acceptable, with scriptures being twisted to justify it all.

Closer to home, we are shocked again and again at how moving away from long-accepted biblical moorings is introduced as "progress", "freedom", and "deliverance from bondage".

Maybe I just don't understand. Having come to know Jesus Christ personally as a young boy just entering his teens, Jesus has always been very precious to me. For a number of the early years of walking with Him, there were virtually no other young people in our local church. The bicycle ride to the church and the daily hour or two spent alone with Him far out from town formed a bonding deep within that is too sacred to be auctioned on some mean block of flighty speculation. Through those early years, I cannot recall ever thinking His ways too demanding or His sweet fellowship less than sufficient. I feel no different now.

Perhaps only those who have spent time lost in His Spirit can really understand how sacrifice of other things doesn't seem like sacrifice when under the influence of this eternal intoxicant.

To me, it is a sad day when preachers... and/or their wives... and/or their children, lead each other (and those who follow them) into the shallows of worldly desires. However, I understand how this is inevitable if the fires of holy hunger burn low, or the naive disciple is led astray. In the final analysis, it is only a hunger for God that brought us into this covenant relationship with Him, and only that same hunger will sustain it. When it burns low, eventually rationalism, earthly interests, mistreatment at the hand of others, or some other such, will push one over the brink of safety.

I am not interested in fighting people or trying to "prove a point". My feeling is, if one doesn't want to live for God, then don't. Unless the Spirit draws a person, he can't live for God anyway. However, there are some things I don't have to guess about. Some things are plainly written in God's Word. Other things about God are spiritually discerned through experiencing moves of the Holy Ghost. There is simply no other way to describe it. The deep, penetrating, searching, purifying, energizing Spirit of God, which moves in waves of glory across a congregation, does things in five minutes that human ingenuity cannot accomplish (nor understand) in five years. When people are exposed to this living experience of the Spirit, one of two things happens. Some are quick to remove themselves from this intensely personal atmosphere. Others, feeling their spirits drawn by this long sought bonding with their eternal Father, are swept into the sweetest relationship known to man. Only when the ardor of this divine love-affair wanes does the world, once left behind, regain its old appeal.

I cannot account for the whole world, nor am I interested in trying to do so, but that does not prevent there being a deep, deep, desire for my children and the local church I pastor to experience the richest of God's blessings. I want them to know the glory of God. It is important for them to experience the surge of God's Spirit as it inundates their body, soul, mind, emotions, and spirit. I will leave it to others to try to downplay the place of experience in knowing the living God. I'm aware that balance is necessary. However, coming from a lineage of "Pentecostals" which reaches back to "Azusa Street" after the flesh, and back to the Day of Pentecost after the Spirit, I also am aware that God is alive, and to know Him is to encounter and experience His presence.

Finally, I know that a holy God is somewhat jealous, and that even little things are significant to Him. We will talk more about "significance" later. However, when God speaks, we should beware of those who (one way or another) say "it doesn't matter", "that's not important", or in some other way attempt to remove responsibility to heed the plainly written Word of the Lord.

Chapter 3

The Process Of Discernment

I use to think that there was such a thing as "total objectivity". I thought judges judged things purely on the merits of the case, without regard to repercussions and without personal biases. It was years later before I realized that, even if one tries to do the above, it seldom is accomplished.

In religious circles, when it comes to shaping one's theology, this declaration of seeking total objectivity often sails under the banner of being totally honest - as in, "I am going to make a decision on this theological issue by being totally honest and completely objective".

Try as we may, we cannot separate ourselves from the variety of forces and flavors that have shaped us and accompanied us to where we are. It is an immature mind that thinks he or she is totally objective. If one clings to this idea into their later years, they end up fooling themselves, and in effect create their own little illusory world to live in.

There are several things that should be taken into consideration when attempting such. On a broader scale, what is, and how do you define, "totally objective"?

One way we make decisions is by basing them on conclusions which we draw from that which we personally have come in contact with. Obviously, conclusions drawn from such experiences are not always based on complete knowledge or objectivity. Another way we add to our store of knowledge, and by which we make so-called "objective" decisions, is by including the experiences, feelings, and conclusions of others in our decision-making process. This, of course, includes their biases, etc. Again, this input is no more purely objective than was our own. Also, we can add to the above our "intuitive feelings" and innate sense of what is true. Again, I think all would agree that this addition doesn't do much to add objectivity to the process.

I propose that most decisions on theological and doctrinal issues which have ethical and moral content (i.e., deal with life-style) contain heavy doses of hidden causes which greatly influence the decisions reached. These hidden causes may vary greatly, and may include such things as sub-surface personal desires, reactions to feelings of rejection, a desire to please ones loved ones, self-pity, or disgust over hypocrisy. Oftentimes, unresolved resentments and unfulfilled ambitions also come into play.

Whatever the cause, sudden convulsions on long-held ethical and moral issues are seldom (if ever) the result of "pure objectivity" or "being honest".

An extreme example of this is people who readjust their doctrine to allow tolerance for immorality.

Years ago, I sat and listened to an older preacher friend of mine expound his convoluted doctrine of repentance. Perhaps, because I was kind and respectful of him, he didn't suspect that I knew of his long list of reputed moral sins. Had he openly confessed to me his failures, he could have hardly revealed himself more completely than he did by simply explaining to me his grotesque doctrine of repentance, and how it worked. Rather than his doctrine shaping his lifestyle, his lifestyle had shaped his doctrine. I can think of few things more deadly.

In using the example above, there is no intent to paint everyone who suddenly changes their doctrine as being immoral, for that is not true. Nevertheless, when doctrines are formulated in flagrant disregard of plain statements of scripture, and when great lengths are gone to in explaining away such scriptures and their relevance for today, then red flags of caution ought to start going up everywhere. Somewhere along the line, the balance so necessary for sound decision-making has been thrown off.

Though it may not be apparent on the surface, there is almost always unseen spiritual, emotional, and/or circumstantial forces at work. The tragedy of such is that unsuspecting friends can be drawn into error while not being aware of the true sources of these "new revelations".

How does one be sure of his/her positions and decisions? To answer this question, we must be aware that the subject of theological decision-making on ethical and moral issues is very important, but also very broad and general. Many volumes can be, and have been, written on these matters. However, some guidelines may be helpful.

First, correct life-style decisions for the christian cannot come out of a carnal mind. The carnal mind is argumentive, combative, and is at enmity with God. It is not subject to the law of God, neither can be. Paul states that, "they that are after the flesh do mind the things of the flesh" (Rom. 8:5). The word "mind" means to "think, decide, judge, or set one's mind on" (Gr. phronousin). It refers to a "disposition of the mind".[6] Thus, they that are after the flesh have a "disposition of the mind" after the flesh.

It is not always easy to know where the initial inclinations toward decisions to change particular ethical and/or life-style decisions come from. It would be a grave omission to fail to inquire whether deep, patient, and holy cleansing of one's self in prayer and surrender to God preceded and accompanied such decision making. The results of deep and real communion with God, and resultant washing in His love, can have profound affect on how one views a particular issue. Such prayer can cause one to discover and relinquish hidden agendas of the heart, which otherwise remain to bend the decision making toward the flesh. Once washed in deep spiritual cleansing, the believer is "after the Spirit", and consequently has a "disposition of the mind" toward the things of the Spirit (Rom. 8:5).

At the risk of seeming redundant, the importance of understanding how much difference the mind-set makes when undertaking to discern truth can hardly be overemphasized.

Scripture is clear that there are two different worlds with two different kinds of wise men, and two different kinds of wisdom. The book of James declares that there is a wisdom "which does not come from above" (Berkeley), but "comes from the world" (Phillips), and has sources which are both soulish and "demoniacal" (Wilson), and is also called "the wisdom of demons" (SEB). Paul informs us that some would give heed to "seducing spirits, and doctrines of devils" (I Tim. 4:1).

In contrast stands the "wisdom of God". It is "not the wisdom of this world, nor of the princes of this world" (I Cor. 2:6). This wisdom is "hidden" (2:7), and is said to come from "revelation" (2:10), as opposed to earthly logic of "man's wisdom" (2:4).

This wisdom, cannot be tapped into by the senses of the body, nor by pure rationalism and emotionalism (2:9). Instead, God reveals them by

His Spirit, which is qualified because it "searcheth all things, yea, the deep things of God" (2:10).

Finally, Paul points out that revelation from the Spirit of God alone reveals the "things of God" (2:11). Spiritual things must be compared with spiritual, because the natural man "receiveth not the things of the Spirit of God: for they are foolishness unto him: neither can he know them, because they are spiritually discerned" (2:14).

Once one ponders the above for a length of time, the value of the Bible also becomes more obvious. Peter speaks of the "precious faith" and the "precious promises", and goes on to declare that the Spirit which inspired the writers was "...not by the will of man: but holy men of God spake as they were moved by the Holy Ghost" (I Pet. 1:1,4,21).

The following story reinforces the importance of careful regard to the Word of God.

Chapter 4

Under The Old Oak Tree

Once upon a time there was an ancient man of God who made a journey to where God's altar was located. There he found a wicked king, standing by God's altar, getting ready to offer incense in idolatry. Anointed by God, the man of God prophesied to the altar: "O altar, altar, thus saith the Lord...", and then proceeded to predict the time when a righteous king would come which would burn the bones of the prophets of Baal on that very altar.

This was a remarkable prophecy, in that it identified (by name) the king who would do this. This king, named Josiah, did come some 300 years later and fulfill this prophecy. What a prophet, and what a prophecy! Furthermore, when the ungodly king attempted to lay hands on the prophet, the king's hand instantly developed leprosy! Only when he requested the prophet to pray for him did the leprosy disappear.

The king was so amazed and humbled by this that he does an about face, and says to the man of God: "Come home with me, and refresh thyself, and I will give thee a reward".

Recognition, acceptance, admiration, power -what more could a man of God want? However, listen to his response: "If thou wilt give me half thine house, I will not go in with thee, neither will I eat bread nor drink water in this place, for so it was charged me by the Word of the Lord, saying, 'Eat no bread, nor drink no water, nor turn again by the same way that thou camest'."

What a prophet! Fearless in denouncing idolatry! Accurate in predicting judgment! Courageous in avoiding the web of worldly approval! Possessing a deep understanding that God's Word is explicit, he is *very* conscious about obedience. Fear cannot stop him. Intimidation is powerless against him. Political power doesn't faze him. Popularity cannot turn him.

Now, in strict obedience to God's Word, he is on his way home. His face is set. His step is resolute. He has resisted all attempts to deter him from the will and Word of God.

However, after being long on the journey, he begins to grow weary. The anointing has settled back like a dove at peace. The adrenalin of the great victories has receded. He is now alone. He feels alone. His sense of fierce urgency has slackened, and his steps become slower. Surely a little rest, a little slackening will be alright.

Finally, he spies an old oak tree, where he stops and sits down. Although the journey is not over, he relaxes and takes his ease. The old oak tree is a luxury, and luxury is something he's not use to. Earlier, as he journeyed in his single-mindedness of mission, he perhaps hardly noticed the trees, the terrain, or anything else. Now, growing tired, he feels himself becoming more acclimated to his environment, and one with his surroundings, and frankly it feels good to have a little freedom from the pressure of the mission. He knows the mission is not complete until he gets home. However, this oak tree sure feels good, and tarrying here for a little while certainly can't hurt anything. So he thinks.

In the distance, he sees a mule and rider. Through the shimmering heat, the rider comes to the oak tree, straight to the man of God, and asks: "Art thou the man of God that came from Judah?" The man of God replies: "I am".

The man of God then gets his *second* invitation to dine, as the rider says: "Come home with me, and eat bread". Though tired, lonely, and hungry, the man of God nevertheless repeats: "I may not return with thee, nor go in with thee: neither will I eat bread nor drink water with thee in this place: For it was said to me by the Word of the Lord, Thou shalt eat no bread nor drink water there, nor turn again to go by the way that thou camest".

"There!", he thinks, "that should settle that." Unexpectedly, however, there is a new element injected into this situation. His new "wants-to-be" host explains to him that: "I am a prophet also as thou art".

Now, this is different. This isn't some reprobate king luring him to disregard God's explicit instructions. This is "one of the brethren". Surely, this is different! Further, this brother explains: "...an angel spake unto me by the Word of the Lord saying, bring him back with thee into thine house, that he may eat bread and drink water". This new guest is a prophet also! He speaks with angels! He has a *new word* from God which offsets the old one! All of this is done just for you, tired man of God! However, all is not well.

There's only one little problem summed up in four words - *"He lied to him"*! It all sounded good, but it was a lie. It was all a fabrication of a dysfunctional mind. This rider really was a prophet, but he hadn't really spoken with an angel. He really was (at times) used of God, but God really didn't tell him to bring back the man of God, nor did God tell him to feed him or give him drink. It was all a lie - a deceit-filled diabolical lie.

We will never know, in this world at least, what motivated this prophet to lead the good man of God which he found under the oak tree to his destruction. What would spur a prophet to such an insidious deception? Regardless of what it was, we know that the man of God became victimized by another's dysfunction that drove him to dishonesty, and took down with him the one who accepted his seemingly logical arguments. With all of his successes and admirable traits, the man of God should never have stopped under the oak tree and listened. He had God's Word, and knew that he did. Instead of holding to it, he listened to another who, in effect, said that "what you thought God had told you earlier has now been changed, and I am sent to tell you the new stuff". "But, he lied unto him".

The "rest of the story" is history - sad history. The man of God, sent with a message and a ministry, listened to the prophet's lie. In place of the sometimes lonely journey in God's service, he accepted fellowship with one who was overtly irreverent, and to whom little was sacred or holy. His new friend was more than willing to sacrifice truth for fellowship, and said that it would be o.k. "But, he lied unto him".

So our man of God backs up to go with the deceiving prophet. "So he went back with him" is the exact language of scripture. He goes with "...the prophet that brought him back". To fellowship him, he has to go back. He eats and drinks with the him in his house. While doing so, the real Word of God comes on the irreverent prophet, and judgment is pronounced on our friend. "Thus saith the Lord, Forasmuch as thou hast disobeyed the mouth of the Lord, and hast not kept the commandment which the Lord thy God commanded thee, But camest back, and hast eaten bread, and drunk water in the place, of the which the Lord did say to thee, Eat no bread, and drink no water; thy carcass shall not come unto the sepulchre of thy fathers".

The man of God leaves. While on the road home, a lion attacks him and kills him. The prophet who deceived him hears of it, and goes and gets him and buries him, "and they mourned over him saying, Alas, my brother!" Did the prophet feel remorse that he had led him astray? Not that is recorded. No remorse. No acceptance of blame. No shame. However, there is this interesting verse: "And when the prophet that brought him back from the way heard thereof, he said, It is the man of God, who was disobedient unto the Word of the Lord..." (I Kings 13:26).

Earlier, we saw that in its infancy, christianity, with all its uniqueness, was spoken of as "the way". The verse at the end of our story states that the deceiving prophet "...brought him back from the way" and said, "It is the man of God, who was disobedient unto the Word of the Lord...". When he left "the way" and "went back", he was disobedient. Disobedience brought judgment. Judgment ended a good ministry (story is taken from I Kings 13:1-30).

So it is that the only reliable guide we have to good ministry is "the Word of the Lord". While many can claim to hear from God (and many do hear from God), all audible messages from God are subject to the written Word of God. All "post-biblical" messages are plainly declared to necessarily be judged by the hearer before being acted upon (I Cor. 14:29). In contrast, the written Word judges the hearer, and is not to be judged by the hearer.

In closing, may I say that I think for many of us, like the servant who was in the master's house because of hopeless indebtedness, our "six years are up". However, rather than run prematurely out of the master's house, we have carefully thought it through and came to a conclusion. Even now, if you will look closely, you will see us on "the way" - the way, that is, to the master's doorpost. There, with a deep love in our hearts, and an abiding trust in the master, we lean against the doorpost, where we are fastened to HIS house forever. For me, that decision was made long, long ago.

In the following pages, we will attempt to assist the sincere christian in the challenging task of better understanding what it means to be the people of God and the temple of God. Just as old wineskins have lost the elasticity necessary to hold new wine, so carnal man and carnal religious organizational frameworks are not fit temples of the Holy Ghost. The "born from above" believer becomes God's temple, and as such is given much instruction in God's Word to enable them to be a worthy vessel.

Corporately, the body of believers is also termed God's household (Eph. 2:19), and likened to a building (i.e., temple) fitly framed (Eph. 2:21). The believer's body is said to be the temple of God (I Cor. 6:19). God is said to "dwell" in the believer (Rom.

8:9,11; II Cor. 6:16), and to "dwell in your hearts" (Eph. 3:17). Perhaps Paul sums it up best.

"And the very God of peace sanctify you wholly; and I pray God your whole spirit and soul and body be preserved blameless unto the coming of our Lord Jesus Christ" (I Thess. 5:23).

The Bible is a very wide, very deep, and very encompassing revelation from God. It is certain that no one has ever plumbed its depths and discovered all that God has to say to us. On the other hand, there are many things which we, as the family of God, can know (and do know) about God and His ways. Careful and patient comparing of God's dealings with mankind through the stream of history reveals that there are many identifiable traits, or characteristics about Him which are seen in scripture. There are numerous "attributes" of God which are revealed through statements made in the Bible, as well as by observing God's actions. In studying the Bible, we first attempt to identify these broad general traits, or attributes of God. Once this is done, we then attempt to determine how these apply to us in everyday life, and what is expected of us to align ourselves favorably with these attributes. Of course, the reason that we attempt to align ourselves with God's attributes is because we, as christians, are meant to reveal, through our lives, what God is like. As Christ was the image of God, so we, as the body of Christ, are also meant to reveal the invisible God (Jn. 17:11,22; Col. 1:15,18). With this in mind, we take a closer look at what it means to be God's dwelling place, and what it means to "reveal God" through us.

Chapter 5

The Dwelling & The Glory

The meaning of the Hebrew word, "shekinah" is "that which dwells" (or "dwelling place").[7] Another definition is "the shining".[8]

The "shekinah" is God's glory, and is (and has always been) associated with God's dwelling with His people. The glory of God and the name of God was forever intertwined in the idea of God dwelling amongst men. In fact, in some versions of the Pentateuch, the word "name" is replaced with the word "shekinah", or glory. Scripture reveals that when God dwells with His people, this dwelling always includes His name being amongst His people, and His glory being amongst His people - with His name and His glory being even interchangeable at times. The scriptural thought is that God chooses to dwell with a particular people by putting His name in a special place.

"But unto the place which the Lord your God shall choose out of all your tribes to put his name there, even unto his habitation shall ye seek, and thither thou shalt come" (Deut. 12:5).

In looking further, we shall see that this idea of the glory and the name being an integral part of God's dwelling is as prominent in the New Testament as it is in the Old. Whatever tabernacle (or temple) God may choose to dwell in, this dwelling will always put His name and His glory in that place.

Time spent studying what scripture reveals about "the glory of God" is time well spent. Our purpose here is to focus on the fact that the shekinah glory of God was always manifested particularly in whatever place God chose to dwell. When God chose a place to dwell, this of course made that place "the sanctuary" of God. Although God made appearances in many places in scripture, He nevertheless chose specific places to dwell. It is to these places that the shekinah glory is especially attached.

In preparing Moses and Israel to be His special called out people, God specifically commanded Moses to build a tabernacle for God to dwell in. God's Spirit dwelt therein in the most interior part of it - the Holy Place, or Holy of Holies. This was where God's glory was. The candlestick in the outer room was always lit as a reminder that the glory was present. The shekinah burned, or shined, on and over the tabernacle as a "pillar of fire" by night and a shining "cloud" by day. This visible glory above the tabernacle was a sign that God was dwelling among them. When the glory was gone, God was gone. Thus, in the days of Eli, "Ichabod" was written over the door, for "the glory had departed".

After entering the land of promise, the Israelites eventually built a more permanent dwelling place for God. Though God is everywhere, and even the "heaven and the highest heaven" (I Kings 8:27) cannot contain Him, God still chooses to dwell and place His shekinah among His people.

The third prominent dwelling place of God among men was in the body of Jesus Christ. Again, we see the same characteristics - this was the place where God could be met, and where God chose to put His name and His glory. For example, when the angel appears to Mary, he declares that the "power of the Most High will overshadow you" (Lk. 1:35). The Old Testament uses this same word (in the Septuagint version) in Ex. 40:35 to describe the shekinah glory of the Lord in the tabernacle. Further, when the shepherds were in the fields, the "glory of the Lord" shone about them (Lk. 2:9).

Later, when Christ was transfigured, and Moses and Elijah appeared with Him on the Mount, scripture declares, "they saw His glory". Scripture also notes, "they entered a cloud" and "a voice came out of the cloud" (Lk. 9:32-35). In addition, the subject discussed by Moses and Elijah was of

Christ's departure when He would, "enter into His glory" (Lk. 9:32, 24:26). Later, Peter, remembering this incident describes it.

> *"For he received from God the Father honor and glory, when there came such a voice to him from the excellent glory..." (II Pet. 1:17).*

From all of this, we can see the emphatic connection in scripture between the glory of God and the temple of God. No scripture writer gives clearer proof that the glory of God dwelt on (and in) Christ as the temple of God than John. John starts early to drive this truth home in the opening chapter of his book by stating of Christ (the Word), "The Word was made flesh and dwelt (tabernacle - i.e., where the shekinah is) among us, and... we beheld his glory". Christ here is shown to be the new, living tabernacle where the glory and presence of God now dwells on the earth. Christ clearly states of Himself that He is the temple of God.

> *"Destroy this temple and in three days I will raise it up" (Jn. 2:19).*

Here, He was speaking of the temple of His body (2:21).

Time and space does not permit us exhaustive study on how the shekinah was in and on (and in fact was) Christ. Anyone familiar with Hebraic expression will not fail to see reference to the shekinah in statements of Christ (e.g., "I am the light of the world" Jn. 8:12). Christ prays that His followers may "behold my glory which thou has given me" (Jn. 17:24).

An important point to note is that when the glory is present it has ethical consequences. Patterns of conduct which were common in the absence of the glory are patently unacceptable when the glory is present. For example, prejudice was part of the society and culture in Bible days. However, James declares that when one holds the faith of our Lord Jesus Christ, they are to show no partiality, and that such boundaries are inappropriate, because when Christ is there, the "Lord of glory" is there. The shekinah, dwelling in the midst of God's worshipping people, demands that the worshipper's conduct be examined and adjusted to be acceptable in a place where the glory is. Of course, in a place where the glory has been cut off (or never was) the congregation would be unimpressed with such things.

From the above, we have also seen that where the glory is there is "a shining". This shining always comes from the interior and is almost always visibly seen above (or over the top of) the temple. The shekinah was over the tabernacle as a cloud by day and pillar of fire by night. In the temple it emanated from within so strongly at times that the priests could not minister. In Moses, the glory shone from within, and again we see it shining primarily through his face. His encounters with the glory were so powerful that it made the courts of Pharaoh, in all their earthly glory, dim and unattractive.

When God's power was working among His people, this light (or shining) could not be contained. The light inside, as also happened with Christ, actually lit up the whole tabernacle. It transfigured the coverings so they became radiant. Day or night, the children of Israel knew that God was in their midst, for this tabernacle could not contain God's glory nor could the curtains hide His glory. What happened to the face of Moses, when Moses had been in the presence of God, must also have happened to these curtains. The tabernacle was transfigured.[9]

The burning (shining) bush, the face of Moses, the tabernacle, the temple Solomon built, the body of Jesus transfigured - all of these repeat the theme that where God dwells, the glory emanates from within and becomes that which gives the outer parts its beauty. In fact, scripture is very specific that the outer part of the dwelling place (whether it is the tabernacle, the body of Jesus, or the New Testament believer), which the world sees, is intentionally left unadorned with artificiality. Man's art and use of earthly materials to create "glow" or color was expressly forbidden, as the beauty of God's glory was greater, and would only be distorted by such artificiality.

It is likely that, being as the New Testament believers are going to be like Christ when transfigured, the "white robes" spoken of in the book of Revelation are actually the glory of God covering the believer with God's glory as a covering. It is evident that this is heaven's wardrobe, for the

46

angels are repeatedly spoken of as "glistening", etc., as well as redeemed men such as Moses and Elijah which appeared on the Mount of Transfiguration with Christ. It is also likely that Adam and Eve were not "naked" when dwelling in the Garden of Eden prior to the fall. The fall stripped them of their glory. Christ uses this terminology in His story of the Good Samaritan - which is the story of the fall of man. The wounded man by the wayside represents the human race, which has been victimized by a "thief and a robber" (i.e., the devil). Christ describes him as having been "stripped" and left "half-dead". This is precisely what happened to Adam. His Spirit died (Gen. 2:17) even though his body-soul continued to live - thus he is "half-dead." He is also "stripped" of the glory of God, and thus left naked. When God clothes him with skins, it is mute testimony that man has lost the glory, and through death, the long process of the restoration of the glory, and hence the return of the emanating covering, has begun.

Ultimately, that glory returns through the work of the "second man" (I Cor. 15:47) which is Christ. Through Him, the human spirit can be "re-born" (Jn. 3:5), and man made whole again. In Him, the seven-fold glory of man (power, riches, wisdom, strength, honor, glory, and blessing - Rev. 5:12) is restored.[10]

The exciting part is that those who are "born again" by birth of the Spirit are "joint-heirs with Christ" in His glory! (Rom. 8:17).

Pondering the above truths make the fashion of this world seem quite drab. Only those who do not dwell in the glory can become entranced with the artificial trinkets of this world, which fashion passeth away (I Cor. 7:31). Those who have partaken of and live in the glory are on the "cutting-edge" of "cosmic fashion" - and have already tasted the "powers of the world to come"! (Heb. 6:5). Those dwelling in such fashionable glory (clothing with divine luminosity) are difficult to convince to become interested in the old fashions of the world which are rapidly passing away. Only if the light in the temple has gone out, or grown exceedingly dim, can one believe this evil world's fashions are attractive.

This did happen. That is, the glory of God did depart from the temple.

The prophet Ezekiel was given a vision of the shekinah glory of God (1:28). Later, he finds himself moved by God from Babylon (the land of captivity) back to Jerusalem, and into the temple built by Solomon. Upon arriving there, God showed him that the people had removed the brazen altar and replaced it with an idol (8:5). He was then instructed to go to the side of the temple and dig through the wall (8:8), which, by so doing, brought him into the Holy of Holies. He was then instructed: "Go in and see the wicked abominations that they are committing here. So I entered and looked, and behold, every form of creeping things and beasts and detestable things, with all the idols of the house of Israel, were carved on the wall all around" (8:9-10).

When the people moved back into these old things of the world, God declared judgment. The slayer was instructed to "smite: let not your eye spare, neither have ye pity" (9:5). He was further instructed to "begin at my sanctuary" (9:6) and "defile the house, and fill the courts with the slain" (9:7). When Ezekiel protested, God emphatically replied: "...mine eye shall not spare, neither will I have pity..." (9:10).

All of this was bad enough, but Ezekiel then stands mesmerized as he watches the shekinah glory of the Lord move out of the Holy of Holies into the courtyard (10:3,4). For years, the Holy of Holies was filled with the light of God's glory. Now it was suddenly put into an abysmal blackness because its source of illumination was gone. "The glory of God moved out the front door".[11]

From there, Ezekiel watched as the glory winged its way into the distance. First, it left the Holy of Holies and dwelt briefly in the courtyard (10:3,4), then it moved to the outer wall and stood at the east gate (10:18,19). It then moved "...from the midst of the city, and stood upon the mountain which is east of the city" (11:22-23). This mount is the Mount of Olives. "God could not reveal His glory in a desecrated temple, so the glory moved from the Holy of Holies to the front door, to the east gate, then left the temple to the Mount of Olives, and then disappeared entirely."[12]

Although Ezekiel prophetically sees that the glory will return to the house of the Lord (43:1-5), it was many years before it did so. That temple was destroyed, and God's people went into captivity for 70 years. As is always the case, when the glory of God departs, bondage always results. At the end of the seventy years, Zerubbabel tried to rebuild the temple. He did succeed in getting it erected; however, the old men wept, and the prophet Haggai conceded that it was no match for the former temple of Solomon "in its former glory" (Haggai 2:3). Furthermore, there is no record of the glory of God ever occupying this new temple. All that is left is a promise from Haggai.

"I will fill this house with glory" (Haggai 2:7).

"This house" that Haggai speaks of is a prophecy of the coming of Christ.

We will pursue in more detail later how the scriptures show the present day child of God to be the temple of God. However, in the light of the above, we are reimpressed with how empty and dark is the temple when the glory is gone. It is only an empty shell, lying in the darkness of light and life gone out. The glory only remains on the child of God as they remain "in covenant" with God. In our time, this can only be maintained by living life in the midst of God's presence, and in careful walking in His Word. Again, when I see those who irreverently trivialize God's Word and work to undermine it's significance for us today, I cannot help but pray that God helps each believer to understand that in being the temple of God, every part of our life and being belongs to God, and is meant to exude His glory.

As we have seen, when the angels announced to the shepherd the coming of the Savior, "the glory of the Lord shone around them" (Lk. 2:9). The glory Ezekiel saw move out of the temple reappears here in the New Testament! Not only does the glory appear, but the Wise Men of the East also see a star. They declare: "...we have seen His star in the east, and are come to worship Him" (Mt. 2:2). Is it only coincidence that Ezekiel saw the glory depart east-ward, and when he sees it prophetically returning, it returns to the temple from the east?

"...and lo, the star, which they had seen in the east, went [Gr. 'was going'] before them, till it came and stood over where the young child was" (Mt. 2:9).

It seems they simply followed the star to Bethlehem. Here, "the shining" makes its way through a universe of constellations, and past all of man's great cities, and finds its way to the humble village of Bethlehem, identifying a particular house in which lies the new temple of God. There it stops and glows above the house as if to say, "the glory has returned".

We have done this review of the glory of God because it is very important to us. As we have seen, God's dwelling, God's name, and God's glory are always together - and in some respects synonymous. The New Testament makes this subject of utmost relevance when speaking of the believer."Ye are the temple of the living God" (II Cor. 6:16)

Just as in the Old Testament, the New Testament also emphasizes that God's glory dwells with, in, and on His people.

"To whom God would make known what is the riches of the glory of the mystery among the Gentiles; which is Christ in you, the hope of glory" (Col. 1:27).

We "behold the glory of the Lord", and "are changed into the same image from glory to glory". How is this done? It is "...by the Spirit of the Lord" (II Cor. 3:18).

In God's dwelling places, His glory has been repeatedly seen as being in (and shining above) each of the places that He chose. For example, in the tabernacle, His glory appeared as a shining pillar of fire. In Christ, the shining appears above the house where He lay as a babe, and later the "dove of glory" descends upon Him at His baptism by John.

As God extends His dwelling place one more time, (that is to the disciples in the book of Acts) the pattern continues to hold true.

"And when the day of Pentecost was fully come... suddenly there came a sound from heaven as of a rushing mighty wind, and it filled all the house where they were sitting. And there appeared unto them cloven tongues like as of fire, and it sat upon each of them" (Acts 2:1,2,3).

That is a remarkable statement! Here we have the shekinah-glory, fire-shining presence of God settling upon these disciples (*not as a group, but upon each one of them individually*!). It "sat upon each of them". Others translate it "separating and resting on their heads", or "distributing themselves over the assembly". When comparing this with the other places in which the shekinah descended, it is not incorrect to assume that the whole room where they were lit up. It is even more certain that each of them were "lit up" with the glory of God.

It also seems significant that before the shekinah descends upon them, Christ first was "received up into glory", and "a cloud received Him out of their sight" (Acts 1:9). The way He is received up into glory is in a cloud! Were it at night, perhaps it would have said a "pillar of fire". Furthermore, when He returns, the disciples are informed that He is coming back *in like manner* (i.e., in "the clouds of heaven with power and great glory - Mt. 24:30).

After the glory cloud leaves with Christ in it, only then can it return to rest upon each of the Spirit-baptized believers as the dwelling place of God's name and glory. Thus, Christ instructed the believers before He went away: "It is expedient for you that I go away: for if I go not away, the Comforter will not come unto you; but if I depart, I will send him unto you". In the meantime, we are

> *"...of the household of God; And are built upon the foundation of the apostles and prophets, Jesus Christ Himself being the chief cornerstone; In whom all the building fitly framed together groweth unto an holy temple in the Lord: In whom ye also are builded together for an habitation of God through the Spirit" (Eph. 2:19-22).*

A last point which is foundational to an understanding of the dwelling places of God throughout history is that He is a Holy God, and His dwelling place is holy.

What is holy? There is much written about this. However, the holiness of God is basically comprised of two parts. The primary part is that holiness in God is connected with the idea of His splendor and His majesty. His holiness is connected with His being a glorious God - one with no deformities or hidden discrepancies in His nature or conduct, and one who is as He appears (i.e., having no deceit or "shadow in his nature which appears by turning").

Secondly, holiness includes the idea of separateness. That which is holy is separated unto God, and is sacred by virtue of being used in God's service. In the tabernacle, everything connected with the service was considered sacred. The priests, their garments, the anointing oil, the altars, the dishes and various utensils, and all the parts of the temple itself (including the walls, floor, inside materials, and the outside materials) - all was holy, sacred, set-apart, and never to be used for anything else, nor mixed with anything else. In fact, even the handling of these things had to be done carefully. The carrying of the things of the tabernacle was assigned to certain people, and they, in turn, were instructed to carry them in a certain way. The idea of holy-separateness also carried with it a certain warning not to treat these things as other, common items.

They were distinctive, and a certain respectful distance was to be kept between things used casually everyday and holy things. To carry the Ark of the Covenant, they were not to even touch it. Rings were attached to each corner of it to facilitate staves which, when slipped through the rings, could be used to carry the Ark on the shoulders of specific members of the priestly tribe.

In speaking of Christ, the Bible states that He was "separate from sinners" (Heb. 7:26).

> "...for what fellowship hath righteousness with unrighteousness? and what communion hath light with darkness? And what concord hath Christ with Belial? or what part hath he that believeth with an infidel? And what agreement hath the temple of God with idols? for ye are the temple of the living God; as God hath said, I will dwell in them, and walk in them; and I will be their God, and they shall be my people. Wherefore, come out from among them and be ye separate, saith the Lord, and touch not the unclean thing; and I will receive you. And will be a Father unto you, and ye shall be my sons and daughters, saith the Lord Almighty. Having therefore these promises, dearly beloved, let us cleanse ourselves from all filthiness of the flesh and spirit, perfecting holiness in the fear of God" (II Cor. 6:14-18, 7:1).

It is hard to believe that these strong, unmistakably clear declarations of scripture can be so ignored today by those who claim the name of Christ. In a world in which raw paganistic ideas are everywhere, immorality and ungodly conduct is considered fashionable, and hedonism and glorifying of carnality is on every hand, the church (of all things) should be a place where the glory is treasured and each one realizes they are the temple of God, and therefore are to be kept separate from the world's filth.

With this in mind, we are brought to Paul's statement which reveals to us that, as God's temple, we are constituted of three parts - body, soul, and spirit.

> *"And the very God of peace sanctify {i.e., keep holy} you wholly; and I pray God your whole spirit and soul, and body be preserved blameless unto the coming of our Lord Jesus Christ" (I Thess. 5:23).*

Chapter 6

Holy Spirit & Human Spirit

To have a "sanctified spirit", such as Paul spoke of in I Thess. 5:23, means that your human spirit is set apart to the service of God. To do this, we have to understand that there are characteristics of our spirits - in the same way that their are senses of our flesh. We can, by looking into God's Word, identify what it means for our human spirit to be kept holy, or separate from uncleanness.

Both the Old and the New Testaments emphasize that our spirits are to be carefully in alignment with God's nature and holiness. King David, a man after God's own heart prayed: "Renew a right spirit within me" (Psa. 51:10).

"...let us cleanse ourselves from all filthiness of the... spirit, perfecting holiness in the fear of God" (II Cor. 7:1).

The subject of the workings of the holy Spirit in the human spirit is a very broad subject. There is no questions that we need all the understanding we can get in this very important area. Probably most of the internal problems you and I face today stem from some dysfunction in spiritual formation. It is not possible to deal with such to any great extent here. However, we do need to at least be made conscious again of the spiritual.

Our spirits can be (and are) affected by other spirits - human and otherwise. While many people, including religious leaders, often disdain this fact, it is nevertheless true.

> "Beloved, believe not every spirit, but try the spirits whether they are of God; because many false prophets are gone out into the world" (I Jn. 4:1).

The Bible speaks of the "spirit of antichrist" (I Jn. 4:3), and the "spirit of error" (I Jn. 4:6). There are "ministering spirits" (Heb. 1:7), "unclean spirits" (Mk. 5:13), "evil spirits" (Lk. 7:21), and "the spirit of the world" (I Cor. 2:12).

Important for us to remember is the fact that we can have a spirit and not know what it is! Even the apostles, who walked daily in physical presence with Jesus, sometimes made suggestions or offered solutions to difficulties that came to them from sources that they themselves did not recognize as erroneous, but nevertheless were erroneous. Jesus, in His rebuke of them, informs them: "Ye know not what manner of spirit ye are of" (Lk. 9:55).

This fact of being influenced from a wrong spirit, and being unaware of it, can lead to serious conséquences. It sullies the human spirit, and grieves the Holy Spirit. When Jesus rebuked the disciples for being of a spirit that they were not aware of, and that they were being influenced by, it is interesting to note that they were recommending a way to solve a problem. The problem was one of rejection. The Samaritans had rebuffed them. They were hurt, and their emotions were raw (not a good time to be trying to lead others!). They were desiring a place to stay, and were refused. Their answer to the dilemma was, "Lord, wilt thou that we command fire to come down from heaven, and consume them, even as Elias did?" (Lk. 9:54).

These were "answer men"! "Yes sir, step right up and we will give you the answer!" They even had answers for God in flesh!

There are numerous things about being influenced by spiritual sources that are important. We already see the dangers of accepting at "first flush" those who have quick solutions to everything. We also have observed to beware of those whose solution is to "smash those who oppose us". In fact, in following leaders (or seeking guidance from the written page), the very spirit in which the leader speaks and acts (and the spirit of an author that exudes from a book) should be "check marks" to us as to whether this is something we want to "buy into".

I have often thought how I would not want some of the so-called conservative, religious-right preachers I know to be elected as President of the United States. Don't get me wrong - I would probably agree with them on most of the major moral and ethical issues. I would probably agree with them on the bulk of their interpretation of scripture. I am certain that I would relate with them on appreciation of the cultural and family values which have made our nation great. Some may ask, "Then what would you be concerned about? If you are in agreement on all of the above, what more is there?" My answer is, "I don't trust their spirit".

To clarify, let me say I am not lumping everyone into the description above. Nor is this only true of those on the "right". It is a human problem. Regardless of philosophical, theological, or political bent, you will find this same *spirit* in all groups - not necessarily more in one group than another. I use the "religious-right" above simply because, being in agreement with it on most "issues", it provides a good example that "issues" are not the only thing that count. For as sure as there are issues, there are spiritual forces driving these issues and those promoting them. Focusing on *issues* only is always dangerous. John Calvin, with all his great intellect and theological insight, still ordered the burning of Michael Servetus at the stake - simply because Michael Servetus disagreed with him on scripture. What an irony - a man attempts to keep christian doctrine clean by murdering someone! However great he may have been in other areas, on this occasion, he certainly did not know what spirit he was of - and it certainly was not the Spirit of Christ. Would you think alleged false doctrine is worthy of murder?

When the Samaritans rejected them, James and John had an instant solution - "Fry em!".

There is evidence that they weren't absolutely sure Jesus would go along with this. Therefore, to strengthen their argument, and to give it additional credibility, they did what is normal for debaters and lawyers. They went back and found "precedent". Not just any precedent, but precedent with a famous prophet - no less than Elijah himself! (Lk. 9:54).

This tells us several things. First, it tells us that you can think you're right and still be wrong. Furthermore, it tells us that one can make a strong argument for almost anything - but making the strong argument, or even winning it, doesn't mean it's true. Therefore, we must beware of making our decisions based on the charisma of the speaker or writer. Lastly, it lets us know that arguments can be bolstered by using examples of things others have done which seemingly justify us taking our desired action, but we can still be wrong in spite of all this.

James and John came up with their idea of what was right, while obviously still affected by a recent action (i.e., rejection). They were angry. They were hurt. They felt they were abused and treated unfairly. While others were on the "inside", they were left on the outside. In a word, their decision was made in the heat of emotions, not under the control of the Spirit of God. As a result, to borrow a phrase from Isaiah, they "erred in spirit". In turn, Jesus informs them, "Ye know not what manner of spirit ye are of".

In contrast to James and John, Jesus knows not only what spirit they are of, but He also knows what spirit He is of. Further, He knows what spirit everybody is of. It is this very fact that makes Him careful as to who He commits Himself to.

> *"Now when He was in Jerusalem at the passover, in the feast day, many believed in His name, when they saw the miracles which He did. But Jesus did not commit himself unto them, because he knew all men. And needed not that any should testify of man: for he knew what was in man" (Jn. 2:23-25).*

Someone may ask, "If there are so many spirits, then how can I know truth?" Our immediate answer is, "Walk in the Holy Spirit, and He will lead and 'guide you into all truth' (Jn. 16:13)". While this may sound simplistic, it is not. For, if one is truly "walking in the Spirit", he/she will not fulfill the lusts of the flesh, for the Spirit of the Lord will lead them and guide them. However, if this "walking" is not done with a truly clean, open, surrendered, worshipping spirit - and if the believer is carrying hidden, unsurrendered things in their heart, then it will, of a certainty, affect the transmission of truth to their lives (Mt. 6:12,14,15).

Someone may ask, "Is 'walking in the Spirit' all that is necessary to insure our walk with God?" The answer to this would be "certainly" - if not for mitigating factors. In fact, Jeremiah, in making a prophecy about this very subject, prophesied the coming of the Holy Spirit baptism.

> "But this shall be the covenant that I will make with the house of Israel; After those days, saith the Lord, I will put my law in their inward parts, and write it in their hearts; and will be their God, and they shall be my people. And they shall teach no more every man his neighbor, and every man his brother, saying, Know the Lord: for they shall all know me, from the least of them unto the greatest of them, saith the Lord" (Jer. 31:33,34).

Jeremiah here plainly declares that the Spirit within will cause the believer to have discernment and be able to discriminate "between truth and falseness, thus insuring their ability to know the Lord for themselves". Paul picks up on this.

> "But as touching brotherly love ye need not that I write unto you, for ye yourselves are taught of God to love one another" (I Thess. 4:9).

However, even in acknowledging this inward, spiritual guidance of God, Paul nevertheless is writing to them things that he evidently felt the Spirit had not yet revealed to them, but was doing so through the very act of his writing. He instructs them to study, to do their own business, and "work with their own hands, as we commanded you". One might here ask, "If they were taught of the Spirit, what is Paul doing commanding them?" The answer is simply that he (Paul) and these believers acknowledged the fact that, although the Spirit does indeed guide, God has also given apostles, prophets, evangelists, pastors, and teachers.

"...apostles; and some, prophets; and some evangelists; and some, pastors and teachers; For the perfecting of the saints, for the work of the ministry, for the edifying of the body of Christ" (Eph. 4:12).

Paul does not stop there, but allows that this gift of men of ministry who assist in guiding the believer is not eternal, but is only "till we all come in the unity of the faith, and of the knowledge of the Son of God, unto a perfect man, unto the measure of the stature of the fulness of Christ" (Eph. 4:13). When this time comes, the saying that "ye need no man to teach you" shall find its unqualified fulfillment.

From this, we see now that God has given two major gifts to lead the believer into all truth. One is the gift of the Holy Spirit itself (Acts 2:38). The other is the gift of anointed men to minister to us. (Eph. 4:11,12)

God has also given one more guide. This is none other than the written Word of God.

"And they shall teach no more every man his neighbor, and every man his brother, saying, Know the Lord..." (Jer. 31:34).

In the New Testament John paraphrases this.

"...and ye need not that any man teach you: but as the same anointing teacheth you of all things..." (I Jn. 2:27).

Some have taken this to mean that, once one receives the Holy Spirit, they are totally dependent upon the Spirit only to lead them. They consider pastors and teachers to be unnecessary restraints on their spiritual freedom. They are "free"! As a result, they are like children left alone with long-experienced seducers. Paul states that God gave the church gifts of anointed men for this very reason.

"That we henceforth be no more children tossed to and fro and carried about with every wind of doctrine, by the sleight of men, and cunning craftiness, whereby they lie in wait to deceive" (Eph. 4:14).

These anointed men are gifts from God, and "speak the truth in love", that we may "grow up into him in all things, which is the head, even Christ" (Eph. 4:15).

When John said "...ye need not that any man teach you; but as the same anointing teacheth you of all things", he was striking at false prophets and spiritual seducers who were trying to lead these precious believers astray. He certainly was not teaching that they did not need pastors, nor was he teaching that they did not need the written Word of God. We know this is true, because he declares: "These things have I written unto you concerning them that seduce you" (I Jn. 2:26). Here, he plainly assumes they understand that, as an anointed man of God (in John's case, an apostle), he has the authority to identify false prophets. Further, he has "written" to them with the authority invested in him as one of the New Testament authors. Thus, within these two verses (I Jn. 2:26,27), John identifies the three areas which God has given to provide the believer with spiritual guidance - (a) The Spirit within, anointing them to identify false prophets and teachers; (b) John himself, as an anointed man of God; (c) The things he has written unto them.

One final note on Jeremiah 31:34 is in order. In churches where great emphasis is put on personal, spiritual experience (such as pentecostal churches), scriptures like Jer. 31:34 are often abused, and used to support the idea that we need nothing but "the Spirit" to lead us in every decision - including critical decisions on doctrine, etc. A closer look at this verse reveals that it is speaking specifically of salvation (i.e., "Knowing the Lord"). The idea is that, up to this time, whatever experience people had of God, it came to them from teaching, training, and explanation by others. Oftentimes, family members did this (Deut. 6:1-5). The prophet is here predicting that the day is coming when these people will have their sins forgiven, and rather than being led to God by ritual or instruction, they will literally "know" God experientially. This happening is, of course, well documented (Acts 2:1-4, etc.). What this verse does not teach is that all of life's decisions (doctrinal or otherwise) are simply to be done by some inward intuition. While the Holy Spirit is our inward guide and is a living teacher, God has also given us other gifts to help us discern truth.

Finally, it seems strange that we need to emphasize that, along with the Spirit of God and the man of God, the Word of God is also necessary to be heeded and looked to as our guide. However, this must be emphasized because of those who erroneously quote such scriptures as "the letter killeth, but the Spirit giveth life", and because of those who attempt to prove that certain scriptures have no relevance for us today (we will see an example of this later on).

The fact is, of the three things God has given to lead us, the scripture is the most reliable, and the only which has no potentiality for error. Even though Peter had actually heard a "voice from heaven", he declares: "We have also a more sure word of prophecy; whereunto ye do well that ye take heed, as unto a light that shineth in a dark place, until the day dawn, and the day star arise in your hearts" (II Pet. 1:19). In speaking of the scripture, he goes on to declare: "For the prophecy came not in old time by the will of man: but holy men of God spake as they were moved by the Holy Ghost" (vs. 21).

> *"All scripture is given by inspiration of God, and is profitable for doctrine, for reproof, for correction, for instruction in righteousness" (II Tim. 3:16).*

An Ear To Hear

I can think of few (if any) statements made to the New Testament church that are more oft repeated than this.

> "He that hath an ear, let him hear what the spirit saith unto the churches" (Rev. 2:7,11,17,29, 3:6,13,22, 13:9).

In the late 1960's and 70's, thousands of young people left home to join the "hippie" movement. Dressed in simple clothing, and living just a little above the basic existence line, they filled the land with their cry of "peace"! Their solution as to how to have peace was very simple. They said, "To have peace, everyone should just quit fighting". From this basic idea came the many protests against war efforts, the draft, and other exercises that included violence.

It was a good idea. It was also naive. Consequently, it didn't work. Why?

Ideas, theories, philosophies, and such, are like a house in a storm. If its foundation is weak (or faulty), it will crumble when it is tested. In religion, doctrinal positions face the same fate unless they are carefully based on a broad, deep, and well-considered foundation. It is not too important whether or not the masses "think" the doctrine is solid, for doctrine is not like American currency which continues to function as though it has real value, when in fact it has little, or none. If you believe the Bible is God's Word (as I do), that human beings live forever somewhere, that the Bible is the guide to eternal bliss, and that disobeying it leads to eternal destruction, then it becomes very, very obvious that it is important that our understandings are correct and built on the foundation of God's rightly-divided Word - and not on a "half-baked" philosophy.

The hippies theory (i.e., " the way to have peace is to simply quit fighting") failed because it did not take into consideration all the factors which make for a solid doctrine. For example, it did not factor in the very evident scriptural fact that, not only are men fighting each other, but there is a third sinister force, alien and opposed to both sides of the human conflict. Even though both sides agree to quit fighting, this third force (which is evil spirits) continues to create confusion, doubt, deceit, and malignity. Secondly, they did not have a full understanding of the present, existential state of humanity. They didn't understand that each man inherently has the latent possibility for good or evil, and that these two parts are constantly at war with one another, ebbing and flowing with the spiritual vitality of the person. The dilemma was heightened in that there is only one place to get such information, and that is from God's Word. However, the dilemma deepens.

Studying the Bible is not enough. Knowing what it teaches is not enough. Even acknowledging it as truth is not enough. There is a deep, spiritual substratum in all of this. To discern truth, to "hear what the Spirit saith", and to avoid error is not primarily in the realm of the rational and intellectual. In a way which we cannot clearly divide, there is a real distinction between the soul (mind/emotions) and the human spirit. Only the Word of God can divide this - not as simply a book, but "...as being alive {'quick', KJV} and powerful, and sharper than any two-edged sword, piercing even to the dividing asunder of soul and spirit... and is a discerner of the thoughts and intents of the heart" (Heb. 4:12).

My brother and sister, *you and I need that discernment*! The church today is swirling with all kinds of dangerous ideas and *we need discernment of the "intents of the heart"*! Beware when someone says they have made some novel, "new discovery". "Test the spirits...", says the apostle. Testing takes time. If someone suddenly proposes that major things (which you've held dear for years) no longer have validity, you need to beware!!

If everything chemists, pharmacists, and scientists say they have discovered as cures, etc., were rushed straight onto the market, great harm would be done. In the interest of the people, elaborate processes to filter the new discovery are established. While people stand waiting impatiently for the new product with its claims, those in charge of testing refuse to be coerced into a hurried decision. They know the terrible consequences that have resulted in the past from incomplete testing. Who can forget "Thalidomide" and the devastation this drug caused because of its ramifications were not known before it was used by expectant women. Thirty or forty years later, thousands of people suffer from life-effecting deformities as a result. Certainly, hasty acceptance of the "new" and "novel" was a dreadful mistake. Oftentimes, a product (or a doctrine) can offer some apparent good result in a given area. However, when all the side-effects and repercussions have been observed, it is seen that the product was not good after all. Thus it is important to carefully check "new" doctrines and to "test the spirits" behind them.

We made mention that there is a difference in mentally apprehending something, and being spiritually affected by it. I am proposing that people sometimes latch on to questionable doctrines under the guise of "seeking to be honest", when they are in fact using "intellectual honesty" as a cover for hidden spiritual desires. The results of such dishonesty are absolutely deadly - once one's spirit is sucked into this vortex, the chasm is bottomless. Seldom does one escape its depths. My advice is, if you want to sin, then just go do it - but don't destroy your ability to discern truth from error by tampering with the mechanisms of your spirit whereby you are able to discriminate between good and evil.

Strange things occur when one's spirit falls into the grip of a spirit not of God. Unless deliverance occurs, the results are fatal. There are so many way for one to be caught in a spiritual web which ultimately brings headache.

When Bonnie came to God, she was an exceptionally likable person. She was (and is) bright, articulate, and has a heart of compassion for others. Everyone in the church liked her, and still does. Over the years, she grew in her walk with the Lord. However, over a process of time, she suffered a number of setbacks in her life. Her children got sick. Her husband lost his job. She was taken advantage of on some business deals, and they were victimized by economic downturn on others.

As her pastor, I always seemed to sense a certain amount of fragility in her walk with the Lord. This of course, was only a feeling, howbeit a troubling one. After awhile, I became aware that when I was praying for (or pondering) Bonnie's walk with the Lord, I almost always felt a little pang of fear. In my spirit, I sensed there was some kind of spiritual vulnerability that I couldn't quite identify. She loved the Lord and seemed to overcome reasonably well. Nevertheless, I was certain that Satan was making a bid for her soul, although outwardly there was nothing to put my finger on.

The battle in the unseen world of the spirit is a battle in a world of shadows. Nevertheless, it is very real. I became increasingly aware that a fierce battle was being waged for this precious soul. The enemy, of course, knew it also. Like he does with all of us, he had patiently probed until he found in her a place of vulnerability (if it is there, he will carefully search until it is discovered). He found a place in her spirit which she was having difficulty surrendering to God. In looking back, I think the enemy identified it and started working on it before I identified it. Like a skillful boxer, he would create (or taking advantage of) situations which caused this spot to be exposed, then he would powerfully jab, jab, jab.

My wife and I countered with everything we had. We fellowshipped as often as possible, which was truly a joy. Behind the scenes was much prayer, fasting, teaching, and preaching - including careful instruction on how to avoid getting hit, how to strengthen weaknesses, and the unavoidable results of not following the fight plan and strategies given us by the master strategist of all time.

With all of that, she was getting weaker. Her spiritual energy waned. She began to miss. Appearing somewhat spiritually "punch-drunk", from the battle, she seemed to grow increasingly less interested in whether she won or lost. In many areas, she was o.k., but in this one area of vulnerability, the blows kept raining mercilessly upon her. Finally, she went down.

Everyone has their areas of weakness. Bonnie's (not her real name) was that she reserved the right to question, and eventually resent her plight. Resentment became a certain deep rage about the unfair things done to her. She kept unsurrendered the privilege to feel cheated. She kept in her possession (as her own) the injustices that had been heaped upon her. She couldn't understand how God could allow them to be cheated, or why other situation were not rectified. If God is good, listens, and loves, then where is He when I need Him? The more she dwelt on it, the more it was exposed to the enemy, and the less willing she was to surrender it to God. Jab, jab, jab. (This description is a composite of numbers of people I have pastored who struggled and sometimes succumbed to the "why me/us" question).

I knew God could answer this. In a moment, He could sweep in with the Spirit and so completely set right this thinking that it would be no contest. For Him, it would be as easy as child's play. However, I also knew He wasn't going to do it. I knew that, even for people who keep no vulnerable places unsurrendered, God oftentimes is very slow about speaking. I remembered Job. He was completely surrendered to God, and it still took him 37 chapters before he could get a "peep" out of God. People talk about the patience of Job in reference to his enduring hardship until relief came. The real message is that he endured silence until he finally chided God into speaking. Not only did Job finally pester God into speaking, but he succeeded in getting God to agree with what he (Job) had contended all along (i.e., that his problems were not because of sin in his life - as his friends contended). Job's contention all along was that neither Job nor his friends knew why this had happened. Only God knew, and He wouldn't talk. Thus Job's plaintive cry.

"Oh, that I knew where I might find Him! that I might come even to His seat" (Job 23:3).

"Neither is there any daysman betwixt us, that might lay his hand upon us both" (Job 9:33).

When Job did finally get God to talk, He angrily verified what Job had contended all along - that no man knew why such things happened; and furthermore, God outlined dozens of other things which man doesn't know anything about!

It was this knowledge (how God can be silent when you think He ought to be screaming), that sustained Job until God finally did speak. In the meantime, Job proved that he was indeed committed to a life of faith, even if God never spoke again!

"Though He slay me, yet will I trust in Him..." (Job 13:15).

So I knew God wasn't going to do anything but remain silent. In His gentle way, He refused to disregard the human will which insisted on clutching some unholy resentment instead of surrendering all. Had she relinquished all in a holy contrition, He probably still would not have answered all her questions - but He most certainly would have gently picked up her broken self, breathed new life into her spirit, and given her sufficient strength to proclaim to the whole world, "Though He slay me, yet will I trust in Him".

With no signs of relinquishment of this fiercely held unholy spot on her part, I knew that I couldn't depend on God to resolve this, that I would have to simply do the best I could.

So, I marshaled my best explanations of such things and went to that Sunday morning service, which I don't think I will ever forget. I was determined. I knew I was probably as ready as I was ever going to be. I sensed that this service would be the climax of months of long struggle, and that this Sunday morning would be forever etched as the moment of destiny in this battle.

I gave it my "best shot". It was the devil's turn to take it on the chin. I went through all the standard explanations, and then launched into some things I had not seen before in scripture until a couple of weeks prior. When done with everything else, I went to Romans 8, and pointed out that Paul said: "the creature was made subject to vanity" (8:20). Paul said that this was done "not willingly" (or in other words, we didn't ask for it or like it), but that it was (at least for now) something we were subject to. I explained that the thing we were subject to was "vanity" (in Greek, "mataioteti). It means we are subjected to things that are "purposeless" and "pointless". Quit asking "why?" - for Paul is saying that there are some things that don't even have a "why?"! He goes on to say that the whole creation is subject to this contrariness to the norm, but he emphasizes that it is only temporary. As this scripture relates to sickness, Paul gives special emphasis to physical problems, and then goes on to say that this will end and there will be a "redemption of" all "our bodies" (Rom. 8:23). He further points out that, in the meantime, we are "saved by hope", but that "if we hope for that we see not, then do we with patience wait for it" (8:25). Meanwhile, the "Spirit helpeth our infirmities: for we know not what we should pray for as we ought: but the Spirit itself maketh intercession for us with groanings which cannot be uttered" (8:26). While we may not know the mind of God on these matters, "he that searcheth the hearts knoweth what is the mind of the Spirit, because He maketh intercession for the saints according to the will of God" (8:27). Lastly, Paul declares emphatically that "we know that all things work together for good to them that love God, to them who are the called according to His purpose" (8:28).

All in all, it was a special Sunday morning. Many people expressed how they now understood things that they before had not understood. The capstone of it all was that Bonnie came to me after church! With tears in her eyes, she thanked me for the lesson and expressed how it had helped her.

Feeling good about the mornings' results, I gratefully listened as she expressed herself. Certainly, the enemy had received a dreadful blow from the Word! What a joy it was to see him reeling in the battle for this soul! It felt good to see old slewfoot wincing under the rain of spiritual blows which fell on him from the Word!

However, a strange thing happened. It was like the voice of the Spirit spoke to me and said, "don't be hasty, you haven't won". People were walking all around me. Bonnie was still standing nearby - but it was all secondary to what was happening inside me. I was learning an important lesson as the Spirit moved me and seemed to say, "You won in her mind. She rationally received the lesson. She understands the sound facts of scripture which you have presented. However, you have changed nothing in her spirit". This is not a battle to correctly and persuasively answer the question "why?". What has posed as an intellectual question is in fact a disguised, unholy spot stubbornly clung to by an unyielding, angry, spirit. Victory and right-standing before God can only come to (and through) a broken, surrendered spirit.

Bonnie doesn't come anymore. To my knowledge, she is not mad at anybody at the church. In fact, I'm sure that they are still dear to her, as she is to them.

Is it over? No, it is not over. Will she come back? By faith, yes, she will be back. Her bent to love God, by faith, will eventually win out. It cannot be otherwise. We cannot let it be. Do many come back from these kind of things? No. In fact, very few - but some do, and I'm believing she will be one of them.

In the meantime, I've learned that decisions about doctrine and conduct, in spite of what one may declare, are not made in some imaginary laboratory of "complete intellectual objectivity and honesty", for there is no such thing. They are made in the human spirit, and the results depend upon whether that spirit is really separated unto God from the unholy, or has some unrelinquished secret stain, spot, or wrinkle.

The above account is obviously a highly subjective one. The facts are correct, and the characteristics mentioned are consistent with what we have observed in many other cases through the years of pastoring and attempting to help people in their walk with the Lord. My prayer is that Isaiah is the spokesman for all the precious Bonnie's who struggle with the pitfalls of life.

"They also that erred in spirit shall come to understanding, and they that murmured shall learn doctrine" (Isa. 29:24).

Spirit Senses

As was mentioned earlier, the human spirit has "senses", somewhat akin to the way the senses of the body work. We know that these senses of the body are the means whereby we discover and relate with the world outside of ourselves. We touch, taste, see, hear, and smell things. By these, we relate with objects outside of ourselves in sensible ways, and learn to utilize them for our growth and well-being.

Likewise, our spirits possess certain abilities to relate to things beyond ourselves, including God. For example, our spirits possess the sense of *worship* (Jn. 3:5,6, 4:23,24), and of *hope* (Rom. 8:23-26), thanksgiving, and of *love* (I Cor. 13:13; Gal. 5:16,22).

Prayer also generates out of the human spirit aided by the Holy Spirit (Jn. 4:24; Rom. 8:23,26). *Spiritual revelation* also comes to the spirit of man from the Spirit of God (I Cor. 2:11-15).

All of the above does not mean that the soul (mind/emotions) and body are incapable of participating in those things, for they do. The sensations of the human experience are experienced and expressed throughout one's being. There is an inseparable (by man) interaction within the body, soul, and spirit of man (Heb. 4:12). However, it is in the spirit of a person that worship, faith, hope, etc., begins and finds first expression. This expression then is continued through the soul-mind and the body.

We have already observed that sanctification (holiness) of the believer includes both separation and surrender to God - thus yielding one's life to become His dwelling place. We have also seen that separation includes elements of consecration, cleansing, and anointing (I Cor. 6:9). This separation means that the human spirit is set apart from uses other than for the purposes of God's will and service. Its "senses" are to be reserved unto God.

For example, *faith*, which is a sense of the spirit, is holy. The Bible teaches us that our spirit should always be exercising faith (Rom. 14:23), as opposed to *unbelief*. Unbelief is faith's opposite and is an unholy use of a human spirit attribute. Likewise, *worship* of the true God (Jn. 4:23,24) is a proper, separated, use of a spirit attribute, as opposed to *idolatry* (I Cor. 10:7,14), which is an unholy use. *Thanksgiving* is opposed to *murmuring*, which is classified as an unseparated, unholy, unclean, and unanointed use of the human spirit (Psa. 50:14; Phil. 4:6; I Cor. 10:10).

Prayer is a proper use of the spirit in relying upon God, as opposed to *self-sufficiency*, which is a silent denial of the need for God's anointing (Prov. 3:5; Eph. 6:18; Jude 20). The human spirit, which is separated unto God, will manifest God's *love* and be separated from love's opposites - *fear, strife,* and *hatred* (II Tim. 2:4-7; I Cor. 13; etc.). Also, this love will be translated into love and *concern for others* (II Cor. 5:14; Rom. 9:3, 10:1), as opposed to *preoccupation with self.* From this, we finally see that to have the human spirit separated and surrendered to God is the secret to keeping a happy, joyful, and healthy relationship with God and in turn with ourselves and our fellow-man.

Because all of the things above are in the realm of the invisible, many people overlook the fact that they are the source of spiritual power and character. As a result, their humanness is always less than the robust strong thing it is meant to be. We should make no mistake - being tainted in spirit is an unholy thing that will short-circuit all of life's endeavors.

Chapter 7

Holy Spirit & Human Soul

Like the human spirit, the soul (mind/emotions) also has characteristics and traits which are part of man's makeup. Like the spirit and the body, Paul prayed that the soul also would be "sanctified" (or "set-apart") unto God (I Thess. 5:23; Rom. 12:2; Phil. 2:5). The soul is to be separated to the uses of God in *purity of thoughts*, as opposed to *filthiness* (II Cor. 7:1; Rom. 12:2; Phil. 4:8); and in *sobriety*, as opposed to *lust* and *foolishness* (I Cor. 10:6; I Thess. 5:6). We are instructed that the *bondage of fear* in the emotions is replaced by the spirit of *liberty* (Rom. 8:15; II Cor. 3:17). *Carnal reason* is to be rejected as unclean and unholy use of the mind, as opposed to an embracing of *spiritual revelation* (Gen. 3:4,5; I Cor. 2:9,10). *Carnal wisdom* is considered unanointed, unholy, and unclean, as opposed to the *wisdom of God* (James 3:15,17; I Cor. 1:19-31).

Imaginations are to be "cast down" in favor of the *knowledge of God* (II Cor. 10:5). *Fear* is to be replaced by a *sound mind* (II Tim. 1:7); and *wrath* is rejected for *joy, gentleness, meekness, temperance, peace*, etc. (Gal. 5:22,23).

In our modern society, there are many inventions designed to attack the purity of the mind. There are few sanctuaries left that have not been penetrated by this barrage. Like giant guns pointed at humanity everywhere, the constant barrage of violent and immoral sexual themes used to market products (as well as to entertain) is a constant source of unholiness. Filthy pictures and conversations, hedonistic and atheistic theories, glorifying of sexual sins, and sensual gratification is the order of the day. This bilge of hell is piped into the homes of millions of naive humans via television, as well as literature. This is injected into the thought processes of millions, thus gradually increasing tolerance for and acceptance of destructive, mind-polluting ideas.

The holy mind, heart, and home of the christian should resolutely cast all such from within - maintaining the unmixed joy and purity of Christ. Paul admonishes us to put on the "helmet of salvation" (Eph. 6:17); and Peter tells us to "gird up the loins of our mind" (I Pet. 1:13).

Every mind has a "secret chamber". It is a chamber that no one else can see into. This secret chamber of the mind is to be kept pure, holy, separated from (and untainted by) evil thoughts.

Jesus taught that cleanliness in this inward chamber was the key to also being clean and holy outwardly. His rebuke of the Pharisees was not against their desire to keep the outside clean, but that they were hypocrites who were "clean outside" (as they should be), but inside were polluted (i.e., full of "dead men's bones"). We might note that this inward pollution can also exist in those who have not cleaned the "outside of the cup". The inside of the cup is not clean, simply because one disregards the outside. *All* cleansing has to begin inside. It is here that many unclean spirits hide, waiting like a malignancy for the set of circumstances that ignites their destructive power to destroy the temple. However, nothing is hidden from The Word of God.

"For the word of God is... sharper than any two-edged sword, piercing even to the dividing asunder of soul and spirit, and of the joints and marrow, and is a discerner of the thoughts and intents of the heart" (Heb. 4:12).

The Word sees all dishonesty. It sees all deceit and ulterior motives.

"Neither is there any creature that is not manifest in His sight: but all things are naked and opened unto the eyes of him with whom we have to do" (Heb. 4:13).

"Finally, brethren, whatsoever things are true, whatsoever things are honest, whatsoever things are just, whatsoever things are pure, whatsoever things are lovely, whatsoever things are of good report; if there be any virtue, and if there be any praise, think on these things" (Phil. 4:8).

Chapter 8

Holy Spirit & Human Body

We have already spent considerable time reviewing prominent characteristics of God's dwelling place in man's journey down through history. We have seen that the dwelling place was so closely associated with His glory and His name that the terminology is sometimes interchangeable. The "shekinah" is both the dwelling and the glory of God (i.e., the place where His name is).

The christian, who has the Holy Spirit dwelling within them, has received the glory of God; and when they are baptized in Jesus Name, they have God's name on them (Acts 2:1-4,38).

Just as the Old Testament tabernacle sacrifices were "holy", so the christian is admonished to "present your bodies a *living* sacrifice, *holy...*" (Rom. 12:1).

> "...*let us cleanse ourselves from all filthiness of the flesh... perfecting holiness*" (II Cor. 7:1).
>
> "*Know ye not that your bodies are the members of Christ?*" (I Cor. 6:15).
>
> "*What? Know ye not that your body is the temple of the Holy Ghost which is in you, which ye have of God, and ye are not your own? therefore glorify God, in your body, and in your spirit, which are God's*" (I Cor. 6:19-20).

The above scriptures should not be run through lightly. It is a fact that, in the New Testament, there is a great amount of scripture which has to do with the believer's body! This is not a small subject. The Bible is not like Dualists who downplayed the significance of the body - nor the Gnostics who declared it to be evil. Neither is scriptural teaching like the teaching of the Sadducees who thought the body would cease to exist. Nor does scripture agree with the Epicureans who taught that one should not worry about tomorrow, but to enjoy every pleasurable experience physically available today.

Just as the "senses" of the soul and spirit are to separated unto God and His service - so also the body and its senses are holy. Just as the enemy constantly attempts to compromise the holiness of the soul/spirit, he also attempts to compromise the sanctity of our body with that which is unclean and unholy.

Because the body is to be separated to God, it is not to be polluted by adultery and/or fornication (I Cor. 6:19). It is to be kept *cleansed*, as opposed to *filthiness* (II Cor. 7:1; Heb. 10:22). He who defiles his body, which is the temple of God, shall be destroyed by God, for the temple must be (and is) holy (I Cor. 3:17). Cleansing includes both soap and water, as well as avoiding anything which is destructive to the body (i.e., immorality, alcohol, drugs, nicotine, etc.). Just as filthiness of the spirit (i.e., idolatry, which ironically is likened to spiritual fornication) is condemned by scripture, and just as filthiness of the mind is condemned by scripture, so filthiness of the body is also condemned. Thus, we are to avoid the unholy in every area of our life.

The body is to be separated and kept apart from being yoked with unbelievers. This unequal yoking is taught to be the equivalent of yoking Christ with Belial, light with darkness, and the temple of God with idols (II Cor. 6:14-17). The "worldly" is considered to be unclean (II Cor. 6:17), and the promise of retaining the parent-child relationship between the believer and God is declared to be dependent upon the believer's separation, cleansing, and anointing (II Cor. 6:18, 7:1; I Cor. 6:11).

Here again, it needs to be emphasized that the Bible has much to say about the body and the importance of its being kept separate unto God. I emphasize this because of the three areas we have discussed, teaching on this area is often neglected.

The general instructions concerning the body (whether male or female) is the same, and most of scripture's instruction is inclusive of both. However, there are some distinctive instructions which are evident.

For example, Paul admonishes men to "lift up holy hands" (I Tim. 2:8). Thus, placing an emphasis on what they do (hands = actions) as being common areas of vulnerability to unholiness through actions and deeds. In Bible days, this was a common prayer position, and represented a pure position of surrender of life's problems and separation to God in faith, as opposed to "wrath and doubting" (I Tim. 2:8).

To female believers, Paul gave some instructions concerning use and adornment of the body which he did not give men. Whereas men's areas of concern seemed to be in their actions, the area of concern addressed to the women included outward appearance versus inward beauty. Both of the two prominent apostles (Peter and Paul) admonished female believers to adorn themselves in "modest apparel", and clearly instructed them to abstain from artificially attempting to produce physical beauty by use of accoutrements and trinkets of the world (i.e., jewelry, pearls, etc., - I Tim. 2:9,10; I Pet. 3:3-5).

The teaching was that the female believer's inward beauty of spirit (which resulted from being filled with God's glowing shekinah) was much greater than what these artificial attempts to create outward attraction could produce. This inward glowing beauty of the shekinah was best manifested by not allowing it to be obscured or screened by outward adornments.

That Christ was best seen through the transparency of the believer (I Pet. 3:4) is evident, and is also equally true of male believers. However, in men, as before mentioned, Paul's emphasis was primarily on what they did. While the actions of the women were equally significant, the natural fact of beauty expressed through the woman, in ways unique to her nature, put her in the position of manifesting the glory of God in ways that are exclusive to (and distinctive only to) femininity.

Therefore, God gives specific instructions which both guard and emphasize this femininity, for as the temple of God, she is equipped to manifest God's glory in ways unique from all others.

Genesis chapter one shows that God created mankind - male and female. The characteristics exclusive to each are all needed for mankind, as the image of God, to reflect what God is. This is the purpose of being made in God's image (i.e., to reflect the nature of God). Thus, when the Bible states that Christ was the "image of God" (Col. 1:15), we know that He was meant to manifest the nature of God to the world. That He succeeded in doing this is clear from His statement to Philip.

> "He that hath seen me hath seen the Father" (Jn. 14:9).

In a similar way, both men and women are made in God's image. Because both the feminine and the masculine are necessary to reveal God's image, there is a clear and definable thread that runs through the scripture which always maintains God's insistence on the distinction of the sexes. Examples of this can be found in plain commands to maintain the distinction in something as domestic as home life, or as subtle as how they worship. Some of the areas in which this is exemplified are:

- In creation (Gen. 2:7,21,22; I Cor. 11:8,9)

- In dress (Deut. 22:5)

- In general relational roles (I Cor. 11:8; I Tim. 2:13)

- In marriage roles (Eph. 5:22,25)

- In family responsibilities (I Tim. 5:8; Titus 2:5)

- In the worship service (I Tim. 2:12)

- In sexual relations (Rom. 1:26,27)

- In appearance (I Cor. 11:7,13-15; I Tim. 2:9; I Pet 3:1-8)

The first chapter of Romans makes clear that unrighteousness, in its final state, brings a complete disregard in gender distinction, even to the point of the sexual relations being so blurred that perversion becomes the order of the day. The thinking finally becomes so twisted and tortured that "even as they did not like to retain God {and His ways} in their knowledge, God gave them over to a reprobate mind, to do those things which are not convenient" (Rom. 1:28). Obviously, everyone who violates one of the above distinctions does not necessarily reach such depravity. However, the general thrust of scriptural thought on the distinction of the sexes definitely shows that such things move people (to one degree or another) in the general direction away from divinely instituted propriety. The differences in movement in such a direction is one of degree, not nature. And although an ethical decision which moves one in that direction may be relatively small and seemingly innocuous, one should nevertheless be aware of what "camp" it makes them a part of.

As we have seen, both men and women believers are the temple of the Holy Ghost. In many respects, the instructions regarding keeping the temple holy is addressed to both. However, we have also seen that there are some areas where their very sexual gender provides a distinctive way in which they manifest the glory of God as the temple of God. Someone has suggested that God makes no distinction on the basis of gender when it comes to being obedient to His word and command.[13] That may be true. However, God does make distinction on the basis of gender when it comes to how that gender uses its unique gender characteristics to manifest the glory of God as the result of being the temple of God. Man and woman are not two different kinds of temples, but they are one temple, each of which is given uniqueness, whereby he/she reveals distinctives within the nature of God. This is (from the divine standpoint) the reason for man being created male and female in the first place (Gen. 1:27). To repeat, the masculinity of the male, christian believer is utilized in the Word of God to bring glory to God primarily on the basis of his actions and conduct. The femininity of the female, christian believer is utilized in the Word of God to manifest God's glory in action and conduct also, but she has another element added to this that is in many respects unique to her, and that is appearance. Scripture directly addresses this in three areas - her ornamentation, her dress, and her hair.

Ornamentation

One of the most prominent things we observed in our earlier look at God's dwelling places throughout biblical history is that God's glory emanates from within. God dwelt "with" His Old Testament people, and "in" the tabernacle which was in their midst. In fact, the tabernacle was set in the direct middle of the camp, signifying God's dwelling in the very center of us. Scripture goes to great lengths to establish that, whereas previously God dwelt with them, He now will dwell in them - and they, in turn, become the literal temple of God.

We also observed that the glory of God was visibly seen as it emanated from and through the structure itself. This is seen clearly in the account of Christ on the Mount of Transfiguration where the glory literally "lit up" his body with a "holy glow". Further, the glory not only emanated from within with a holy glow, but was also consistently seen manifested as the shekinah cloud hovering at the top of the dwelling place. This was one of the foremost traits of Moses' Tabernacle. The head of Moses had to be covered because of the glory glow of God's presence. When Christ was transfigured along with Moses and Elijah, Matthew wrote concerning Christ, that His raiment was "white as the light", and "his face did shine as the sun" (Mt. 17:2). Furthermore, just as the shekinah-glory cloud shone over the Old Testament tabernacle, so Matthew declares: "While he yet spake, behold, a bright cloud overshadowed them..." (v.5).

Again, on the Day of Pentecost, "cloven tongues like as of fire sat upon each of them" (i.e., each of them, as the new temple of God had the shekinah-glory shining from within, and a "personal pillar of fire" which manifested that in them "the glory dwelt").

In conjunction with this, we have seen that specific instructions, throughout time, have been given concerning God's dwelling places - the outside was to be left without artificial beautification. The beauty of the outside was always dependent on there being glory on the inside. If the glory was there, it shined through, and by virtue of its presence beautified the outside.

God's attitude has always been, "I will make the place of my feet glorious" (Isa. 60:13), and He hasn't changed now that He inhabits mankind. Man may bring God glory in His superior strength, but He uses women in a distinctive way to fulfill His promise to "beautify the place of my sanctuary" (Isa. 60:13).

> "Whose adorning let it not be that outward adorning of plaiting the hair, and of wearing of gold, or of putting on of apparel; But let it be the hidden man of the heart, in that which is not corruptible, even the ornament of a meek and quiet spirit, which is in the sight of God of great price" (I Pet. 3:3,4).

The above verse is in perfect accord with all of the previous places where we have observed God's dwelling place. As the temple of God, these christian women were instructed that their beauty would be an "emanating" beauty, and that artificially- created beauty would but obscure (or screen) the real beauty. When the glory emanated from the tabernacle, there was no question of its attractiveness. Just as the divinity in Christ created such an attraction that all men were drawn to Him, and through Him to the God of life, so the christian woman, Peter declares, is definitely to be ornamented with a flash that isn't some sparkle from an earthly trinket, but is, as one translation puts it, "unfading loveliness" (Noli); and another says, "is costly" (Concordant), and "...of surpassing value in God's sight" (Berkeley).

The word translated "adorning" is in Greek "kosmos", and is usually translated "world" - meaning the world and the universe. It is presumed that it came to mean jewelry (i.e., "cosmetics") in relationship to the sparkle of the starry sky.[14] Peter is not denying the christian woman the opportunity to have "sparkle", but is revealing that her glowing beauty is not from man-made trinkets, but is rather an interior glory that, as it breaks forth, is luxuriously, elaborately dazzling - in the same sense that Christ's "face did shine as the sun, and his raiment was white as the light" (Mt. 17:2). The christian woman who is joyfully exuding the glory of God doesn't need to wear a jewel, *she is a jewel* - and God gloriously shines through her!

Peter uses the example of Abraham's wife, Sarah, as an example of one who had understanding about the beauty of a woman. As would be normal for any rational woman, she had a healthy concern and desire to be attractive. She knew that to look her best, a woman had to give attention to adornment, and like a wise woman, she did so. From the text, it is obvious that she had given some thought to this, and considered that being adorned to be her attractive best was important. It is also evident that not only Sarah, but other "holy" women in ancient times knew something about how to be beautiful. The text declares that they "adorned themselves", or "sought to make themselves attractive" (Norlie).

Now, it's not like they didn't have competition! These ladies ran in some pretty high circles! They were "competing" with ladies who dwelled in the courts of some of the wealthiest people around - and, believe me, history reveals that these gals in these heathen nations knew how to "lay it on"! Ancient archaeological diggings reveal very clearly that ladies have known for a very, very long time how to utilize every available material and artifice to shade, elaborate, accentuate, eradicate, and emphasize. In fact, of all the serious sciences on the earth, this is probably one of the few in which knowledge today of "how to do it" may be considerably less than it was three thousand years ago. For, you see, those ladies knew how to use this stuff! In fact, I noticed sometime back that someone was actually using Cleopatra's name (probably without permission) to sell a modern cosmetic. This, of course, proves conclusively that my assumption is almost certainly correct that ancient women may have known even more than modern women about the ancient, secret arts of feminine adornment.

These are the kinds of women who were the fashion plates of Sarah's day. Probably not much different than today. Physically beautiful in every possible way. Before going out for the evening it was "tighten this, loosen that - oh, goodness, this is killing me! Help me, honey! I can hardly breathe! Oops, I dropped my glasses, could you pick them up, if I bend over, it'll cut my circulation off".

However, bulimia aside, we know physical beauty is important. Furthermore, when Sarah saw these same courtesans ten or twelve years later, she could already see the small shadows of panic in their eyes, as they looked in the mirror and saw a few new wrinkles here, and a resettling of a few ounces of cellulite there. For whatever is of this flesh is surely going to fade, as sure as the sun goes down. She could see how galling and frustrating it was as they saw yesterdays girls taking their place as the new fashion plates of fleeting, earthly beauty.

It must have been somewhere along here, in her beauty study, that Sarah came upon an exciting discovery - that there is a beauty "imperishable in quality" (I Pet. 3:4, Wuest) and of "unfading loveliness" (I Pet. 3:4, Noli).

Make no mistake, this woman Sarah was beautiful. She was a "knock-out". She had a beauty which made the beautiful women of Pharaoh's house pale in comparison. She was so striking that when she entered, the whole country was in a stir! "And it came to pass, that when Abram was come into Egypt, the Egyptians *beheld the woman that she was very fair*". Not only was the common populace "wowed" by her, but the princes of Pharaoh's court (who were accustomed to beautiful women) saw her, and were so taken aback by her that they went to Pharaoh, and in essence said, "Doc, you gotta meet this woman who just came to town - she's unbelievable!" (Wilson's paraphrase of Gen. 12:15). Her husband was so conscious of her beauty that he literally worried that someone was going to see her and kill him to get her (What a wonderful dilemma! - Gen. 12:12). He actually discussed this with her over dinner (or somewhere), and explained to her that he was about to enter into Egypt. Therefore, "he said to Sarai his wife, I know that you are beautiful to behold" (Gen. 12:11, Amp.).

It is this striking, beautiful, dazzling, head-turning woman that the Holy Spirit inspires Peter to use as an example of the kind of beauty which emanates from within the holy, christian woman's spirit!

All kinds of things have been said about this. Some have even gone so far as to theorize that because other Old Testament women wore jewelry, Sarah, no doubt, also wore jewelry. I would gently suggest that no less than the Apostle Peter, the very foremost of the 12 apostles, simply states that this is not so, but plainly states that her adorning was an interior adorning as opposed to and exterior (Gr. exothen). Even among today's enlightened thinkers, I would think it very difficult to find a more authoritative source than the Apostle Peter. The truth is, as we shall see, it would not in any way change the truth of the teaching here. For, in regards to that, it would make no difference whether Sarah wore jewelry or didn't wear jewelry. In fact, jewelry-wearing in the Old Testament, rather than exemplify that it should be worn in the New Testament, does just the opposite.

Oftentimes Rebekah, the bride-to-be of Isaac, is used as an example to encourage the idea that wearing jewelry by a christian woman is acceptable, in spite of the fact that the two foremost apostles,

Peter (I Pet. 3:1-6) and Paul (I Tim. 2:9) both teach clearly that it is not consistent with what God has in mind for the christian woman. We will discuss this shortly, but first a parenthetical word from our author.

I want to here remind the reader that in this book's opening pages, the story of an ancient biblical custom is repeated. In this story, we identified who this book is addressed to. We saw that it is addressed to love-slaves - christians who came to Jesus with an unpayable debt. We were basically hopeless, and most of us had little or nothing to boast about. We were not a people, but He took us in and made us a people. We had no inheritance, but He made us kings and priests. Although some had attainments, accomplishments, etc., they were all in areas which were not of "ultimate concern", and hence, were pretty useless in view of eternity. Even though some of us ran into His house as an escape from judgment, after awhile we came to know Him, and fell in love with Him, His house, and His ways. We came to understand that His ways were expressed in His Word, and that you didn't have to be a theologian to understand them - you just read them, and did what they said. We also believed that He had His own reasons for His ways, and that it really wasn't too important for us to worry about the "why's", but that we should concern ourselves with obedience in faith.

Since then, we have been told, in so many words, that (in many cases) we can more or less disregard things we find in scripture which are inconvenient.

Also, if scripture seems to demand anything which would make us stand out as being a little different, then that too can be left out. In fact, we are told that we can be more effective if we consciously work to not attract attention to ourselves by being different, except in ways that are not obvious. Instead of lights on a hill, we are led to believe that we should be underground agents, God's moles, sneaking around in the world incognito, blending with everything so we can launch a surprise attack.

God willing, I will address all of the above. First, we want to reiterate again that God never tries to make His ways to be "rammed down people's throats". Even in the local church, which has both the right and the obligation to have its "house rules" - nevertheless, if one doesn't want to abide by them, they do have (and should have) the prerogative to leave.

However, I'm not interested in anything which moves in even the slightest direction away from the Master's house. For some, the Master's house may be a launching pad to some other place, or opportunity, or way. If that's so, then that's so. In the meantime, I believe in the Master's wisdom, and intend to conscientiously follow Him and His written word. I will take my chances with the Master of the house. The teaching on the scriptures in this book are only intended for those who feel the same.

Now, as the radio use to say, "Back to our story".

In discussing the subject of jewelry, someone has declared that, since Abraham had it put upon his daughter-in-law, Rebekah, then certainly it must be O.K. To this I would say, "If you want to wear jewelry, just go wear it", but using this story to validate it is a mistake. In fact, using any Old Testament example to validate such is a mistake. There are no New Testament examples of wearing it, but rather clear prohibitions against it.

First, we need to be aware that in the Old Testament, the people were not, individually, the temple of God. The tabernacle was in their midst - but they were not the tabernacle/temple. Thus, the prohibition of painting (or otherwise creating artificial beauty) was written in regards to the tabernacle, not the people. In the New Testament, we are literally the temple of God. This is not figurative or predictive of the future, we are it! Here - now - really. Therefore, just as the glory within illuminated the temple of old with sparkling beauty, so the glory does the same in the believer now.

We also need to understand how Old Testament people and events relate to us.

Old Testament characters and events are for our instruction. However, this is done primarily through what we know as "types and shadows". In other words, an Old Testament story can (and many times does) have more than one meaning. It can have its literal meaning, as an actual occurrence at a given time and in a given place, and then also have a typological meaning. As a type, what it is teaching us oftentimes is an ethical or moral teaching that may not be part of the story in actual happening, but is still extrapolated from the story elsewhere in scripture. The way we know the "type" of a given story is that, in most cases, the New Testament types it for us, either in plain statements or by otherwise helping us to see its obvious teaching.

For example, in the book of Genesis, a unique priest is seen by the name of Melchizedek. The book of Hebrews tells us that he was a type of Christ (Heb. 7:15). Another example is seen in the rock that followed the children of Israel in the wilderness. They received the water needed for life from this rock. Paul likens this rock to Christ (I Cor. 10:4). There are scores of types - with Christ, of course, being the central theme of virtually all types.

Some types are so obvious as to be easily observable by even the casual Bible reader, even if not overtly mentioned in the New Testament (Joseph as a type of Christ is an example). Others would probably never be connected without the fact that the New Testament does it for us (e.g., I Cor. 9:10). Always the New Testament counterpart to the type is greater than the Old Testament story from which the type is taken. With this in mind, perhaps, we can better understand the story of Rebekah and her jewelry.

Abraham, who was of course Isaac's father, had grown old, and recognized that his son Isaac did not yet have a wife. He senses that he needs to do something about this. Consequently, he calls his eldest servant to him, and says, "Put I pray thee, thy hand under my thigh: And I will make thee swear by the Lord, the God of heaven, and the God of the earth, that thou shalt not take a wife unto my son of the daughters of the Canaanites, among whom I dwell, But thou shalt go unto my country, and to my kindred, and take a wife unto my son Isaac."

This servant was no "dummy". He considered that he was going to a land foreign to himself, and was to find a beautiful young lady and convince her to go with him, a stranger, to meet and marry a man she had never seen. He recognized this as a pretty big order. He also saw that it may be a challenge to convince this girl to come with him. How was he to find her?

So he responds to Abraham's commission by asking a few questions. He knows there could be complications. So he asks, "Peradventure the woman will not be willing to follow me unto this land: must I needs bring thy son again unto the land from whence thou camest?". The response from Abraham is a very strong, "NO"! He informs the servant that God will "send his angel before thee, and thou shalt take a wife unto my son from thence". In other words, "you are going to have divine assistance in this job". Abraham goes on to say, "And if the woman will not be willing to follow thee, then thou shalt be clear from this my oath: Only bring not my son thither again" (Gen. 24:8).

As is obvious, the story above is a beautiful parallel to the church. It types perfectly all the major aspects of what God is doing in the world today. Abraham is a type of God in His Fatherhood. Isaac is a type of Christ. The servant is a type of the Holy Spirit in the anointed ministry, gone into the world to receive a bride for Isaac/Christ. Knowing how important it is to Abraham that Isaac have a bride, he evidently wonders if perhaps he should take Isaac to her if she refuses to come out of her old world. To this question Abraham emphatically declares, "If the woman will not be willing to follow thee, then thou shalt be clear from this my oath: only bring not my son thither again" (24:8). The one thing the Father will not permit is for the bride to stay in her old world. She must be willing to come out and follow the servant to a uniting with the groom. The servant is thus ordained to go forth and takes solemn oath that he will be faithful to his commission.

The servant finds Rebekah. She is asked, "Wilt thou go with this man? She said, "I will go" (24:58). "And Rebekah arose...and followed the man" (24:61). Her ultimate anticipation was that, at the end of the journey, she would be united with her Isaac, and be heirs together of Abraham, and joint-heir with Isaac (c.f., Rom. 8:17). However, while on the journey to that great day, she was laden with gifts of love. These were given to her by the servant, but were from the Father - "for every good gift and every perfect gift is from above, and cometh down from the Father..." (James 1:17). The servant is like the searching Spirit of God, drawing the bride to the

Father's house to be united with the Son (Jn. 14:1-6). Once she is found, she is heaped with gifts. The servant, as a man, is a gift (Eph. 4:8,11). However, more importantly, the servant represents the Spirit of God guiding her home - for "when He, the Spirit of truth, is come, he will guide you into all truth..." (Jn. 16:13). Thus, from the servant, she receives these gifts of gold and precious jewels. There were "many gifts", but all were from the "same Spirit" (I Cor. 12:4). In addition, she received "gifts of raiment"(Gen. 24:53) Thus, the bride is clothed with the shekinah-glory (i.e., "heaven's jewelry") from the Father.

That gold in the Bible was obviously typological is common knowledge. In every earthly structure that God dwelt in, the Holy of Holies always had virtually everything covered with gold, which represented divinity. Precious metals and jewels have always had typological meaning in scripture of that which is precious, pure, and of great value (I Pet. 1:7; Rev. 3:18; I Cor. 3:12, etc.). Gold, in particular, has represented God from antiquity.

Only in the church age has it finally been possible for God to dwell within the believer in a soteriological way, rather than simply dwelling with man. That there is a distinct and dramatic change in this regard could only be overlooked by the most careless of students. The whole Old Testament is geared to progressively lead up to this time when the divine "gold" of God's presence would no longer be with man, but "in" man. Many, many scriptures emphasize this dramatic and pivotal truth - that the

Spirit within is the fulfillment of God's plan to dwell with man (Jer. 31:31-33; Isa. 28:11,12; Ezek. 37:13,14, etc.). The beauty of God's dwelling place has always been an emanating, interior beauty. Even in Christ, the simplicity of the outward Christ (Isa. 53; Phil. 2:5-8) is quite a contrast to the glory emanating from the inward, divine Christ (Rev. 1:13-18). Perhaps this is why, when Israel made a golden image to represent God, Moses had it ground up, thrown in the water, then made the people drink the water - thus showing again that gold is representative of the divine gold of God within.

One must be careful of casually taking the literal Old Testament happenings and attempting to recreate them in present life. They were not intended that way. Otherwise, being as we are kings and priests unto God, we would be re-creating priest uniforms from Leviticus. If it were intended to be literal then we would get a divine "rock" because Israel did. However, we know "that rock was Christ" (I Cor. 10:4), and so forth. The fulfillment of Old Testament types are spiritual, not literal.

Few things in scripture affect the christian woman in a practical, material, daily way, more than this subject of adorning, including jewelry, make-up, and wearing of appropriate or inappropriate apparel. Because looks and appearances are so important to us (and even to God), appearance sometimes receives more time and effort than it merits. While development of graces of the spirit are given short-shrift, and a compassionate and activist vision of the lost and needy world is lacking, people struggle by the hour over "can I do this", or "should I do that". Why? It is evidently because it hits so close to home - our own views of ourselves, and how we appear, which in turn affects our sense of self-esteem and worth.

To christian women who faithfully and quietly accept and follow Sarah's teachings and findings, there has come a very real awareness of how powerful this inward beauty is. There is a certain luxurious quality to it which is very, very powerful and non-fading; and which, when placed beside the artificiality of this world, causes the latter to appear for what it is - a burden to be put up with. As one woman declared: "I wouldn't be caught without my make-up on. I don't even take out the garbage without my make-up on!" Now that sounds like bondage! This is certainly not meant as an indictment of women of the world who do not have this inward shekinah-of-the-Spirit to depend on to give them beauty. For without the inward beauty, I can understand how a person would feel the need to do something to make up the difference. Being filled with the Spirit is, indeed, the necessary difference.

Some have taught that Peter and Paul didn't mean that one was not to wear "any" jewelry, but rather they should not wear "excessive" jewelry. In the case of Peter, this is justified by saying, "The proof that Peter is not completely banning jewelry is found in the fact that you can forbid the plaiting of the hair and the wearing of jewelry, but the logic fails when you carry it to the third part of putting on apparel. You can't prohibit or ban that part! So if

Peter is forbidding women to wear any jewelry at all, to be consistent he is also forbidding them to wear clothes also".[15]

The exact transliteration of this verse from the Greek is: "whose let it be not the outward of braiding of hair, and putting around of gold, or putting on of garments adorning" (I Pet. 3:3). From this it becomes clear that he is not talking about not wearing clothes (which was obvious already from the context), but rather avoiding unacceptable "adorning" garments. As we have already seen "adorning" comes from "kosmos", which includes the idea of sparkling or dazzling, "attention-stopping" clothing. Lamsa translates it "costly apparel", and another translates it "the wearing of beautiful dresses" (Montgomery).

Paul also addresses this subject in his writings to Timothy.

> *"I will therefore that men pray every where lifting up holy hands, without wrath and doubting. In like manner also, that women adorn themselves in modest apparel, with shamefacedness and sobriety; not with broided hair or gold, or pearls, or costly array; But (which becometh women professing godliness) with good works (I Tim. 2:8-10).*

This verse is a call for sensible and reverent conduct by godly believers. The verse regarding women's adorning is virtually a repeat of the verses which Peter wrote. The emphases are the same, and the prohibitions are the same.

We reiterate that, as always, there will be those who (for varying reasons) will decide not to follow the admonitions of these verses. Again, we repeat that, should someone want to live other than by these very clear and very direct teachings of scripture, that is their prerogative. God has never resorted to coercion to insure that He has a people. It is a mistake for one to think for one second that coercion has anything to do with living for God - for it does not. Besides, were one able to force others to abide by these guidelines, it would mean absolutely nothing were it not coming out of a heart of love for the Master. This is not to say that these things should not be addressed - for they should. Nor is it meant to imply that the local pastor and local church do not have the right and responsibility to adhere to clear teachings of scripture in the operation and management of the church - for they do. Pastors do have God-given authority to teach, preach, and even require. When Titus was left in Crete, he was given explicit instruction that he was there for the express purpose of "setting in order the things that are wanting" (Titus 1:5). He is informed that there are many unruly and vain talkers and deceivers there, and that their mouths must be stopped - for they are subverting whole houses (v. 11).

"Wherefore rebuke them sharply, that they may be sound in the faith" (Titus 1:13).

The Bible is abundantly clear that the ministry has the authority to "reprove, rebuke, and exhort..." (II Tim. 4:2). Timothy is taught that the man of God is given the scripture, and that it "is profitable for doctrine, for reproof, for correction, and for instruction... That the man of God may be perfect, thoroughly furnished unto all good works" (II Tim. 3:16,17). God's ministry was always intended to preach with real authority.

"These things command and teach" (I Tim. 4:11).

People who find themselves, and their families, in a church where the pastor cannot (or will not) proclaim the plain teachings of the Word of God are surely in a precarious place. Like Lot, they may survive the permeating effect of false ideas on their lives. Lot's children, however, could not survive, and became victims of error. Because Lot was evidently cowed by his environment, and attempted to coexist peaceably with its sins, he lost his family. He lost his wife to death. He lost his children to that which was worse than death (i.e., a life without critical faculties of judgment, which is the basic definition of a reprobate). Meanwhile, he seemed to cover his apparent predilection to cowardice with a whining kind of pseudo-peacemaking. If all of this sounds like the place your in, then I suggest you not even take time to pack - just flee for your life before judgment falls.

So, does the ministry have authority? Yes, it does. It has real authority. Not the kind that must be propped up with uniforms and titles, but authority from above. Woe to the man who has it and won't use it to protect the flock, or who uses it dishonestly.

"Cursed be he that doeth the work of the Lord deceitfully, and cursed be he that keepeth back his sword from blood" (Jer. 48:10).

With all of this, God still has granted the individual the prerogative to follow His Word or reject it. There is no place in God's church for intimidation, coercion, or ruthlessness in attempts to bring alignment with scriptural guidelines. This kind of roughness is not only completely unscriptural, but is counterproductive to the desired end - which is to see the individual believer grow up into the fulness of the stature of Christ. A preacher who practices such tactics makes himself unfit for the ministry, and does great damage to the cause of Christ. Ruthlessness is not a fruit of(nor a gift of) the Spirit.

We have here purposely digressed into a brief discussion of the ministry. Our reason for doing so is to try to keep in perspective the various elements which have to be respected to stay scriptural. This is not always easy, nor can it ever be done in the flesh. Nevertheless, scriptural teaching was not written to be ignored and disregarded. However, this is what is being proposed by some.

For example, in regards to I Tim.2:9 it is taught that Paul was using a "Hebrew idiom", and that this idiom is a manner of speaking which would minimize the first clause in order to emphasize the second. Thus, I Tim. 2:9 (according to this idea) should read "Let not a woman's adorning be *only* that of outward things, such as fixing her hair, wearing gold, or pearls, or apparel - but *also* (or *rather*) let it be the inward adorning of a meek and quiet spirit".

Thus, the whole tenor of the verse is changed. What was a stark contrast now becomes only a muted comparison.

The biggest problem with this is it is simply not what the Bible says. It is not there. It is not in the original Greek. It is not in the King James version. It's simply not there. To get it to say that you must add words - which is pretty serious business. My advice would be, don't follow people who make up their own Bible.

In saying this, I do not want to imply that important aids to interpreting scripture are not useful, for they are. However, when the "crutch becomes the leg", then it is being used improperly. Aids can be used to corroborate scripture, but can never be used to replace the scripture itself. When this is done, it opens up a whole mine field of possibilities which lead to all kinds of spurious things. For example, in using the above idiomatic rule to form doctrine, we can really come up with some interesting doctrines. For example Ephesians 5:18 would read: "And be not drunk *only* with wine, wherein is excess, but be filled with the Spirit *also*". Thus, instead of there being a prohibition on being droopy drunk, *we are encouraged to be so* - as long as we are filled with the Spirit also. David Bernard gives another example; "Using this interpretation,

Rom. 13:13,14 would mean, 'Let us walk honestly, as in the day; not in rioting and drunkenness *only*, not in chambering and wantonness *only*, But put ye on the Lord Jesus Christ *also*'".[16]

Numerous other examples can be cited, but are not necessary. The fact is that if the use of an idiom changes the very meaning of a scripture, it obviously is a mistake, and a mistake which wrests the Word becomes more than a mistake - it becomes a heresy. Again, if one simply wants to do different than what the scripture teaches, they are free to just go do it. However, the error is much more grave when we, in effect, attempt to rewrite scripture.

Transparency

We have already observed that the outside of all of God's earthly dwelling places was to be left natural so that the glory within may be seen and recognized as the true source of beauty. The scriptures we have already observed also reemphasize that in the church, the believer is very much the temple of God. In Peter's instructions to christian women, he again shows how Sarah discovered the source of real beauty - and that it was interior. The whole point of Peter's interdiction against outward adorning was that the outward was to be left natural and unmolested, so as to give this sparkling inner ornament the opportunity to shine. Being as this ornament was (and is) the Spirit of God within, when it is allowed to shine, God is glorified. This is one way in which the christian woman fulfills the scriptural exhortation to "glorify God in your body, and in your spirit, which are God's" (I Cor. 6:20). Thus, exterior adornment (of whatever kind) was to be avoided. The point was to avoid anything which obscured (or re-directed attention away from) the emanation of the inward glory. It is interesting that scripture strongly associates outward adorning (make-up and jewelry) with the deceit of seduction and allurement to immorality.

We should here note that scripture has many ways of teaching. One of these is by "association". Scripture uses *representative events* (such as the sacrifice of a lamb) which will incorporate teaching about, not only the lamb as a representative of Christ, but by association other primary things which are part of the event also. For example, not only the lamb has typological meaning, but the altar takes on typological meaning - as well as the blood, the priest, etc. The value and meaning of these secondary items is defined by their use and relationship with the primary subject, which in this case, is the lamb.

There are also *representative places*. The land of Canaan was such a place. Not only was it the actual land that Israel would inherit, but it became representative of entering into the promises of God. The writer of Hebrews uses it to represent God's rest, and equates the believer's lack of entering into God's rest with Israel's lack of entering into the land. Thus, the New Testament takes the land and injects it with representative meaning. Other examples are Egypt (type of sin and bondage); Babylon (confusion, man's world-systems with God left out), etc.

Just as there are representative events and representative places, there are also *representative people*. These are people who become larger than life, and who transcend Old Testament and New Testament boundaries. They, and the characteristics and events which surround them, become the standard (or pattern) by which these particular things are associated and interpreted from that point forward. Thus Abraham becomes the "father of the faithful". Though Abraham is an Old Testament character, he is one of these representative people, and is thus accepted as the standard bearer for faith in the New Testament. Moses is also one of these people. For most of us, hitting a rock with a stick would be a harmless action. Not for Moses, for he is a representative man. When he hits a rock, the incident takes on much larger significance. The rock itself becomes representative of Christ. Again, as was the case with Abraham, the New Testament injects both Moses and the things surrounding him with significance far beyond his very human actions, for he is a representative man.

All representative men were not good. Jude speaks of the "way of Cain", the "error of Balaam", and the "gainsaying of Korah". These men (and the things associated with them in scripture by the Holy Spirit) are forever etched in the halls of immortal infamy as examples of things and ways to be studiously avoided.

Many Old Testament people are used as examples in the New Testament. However, being a representative person is a different thing. It goes beyond just being an example of something. Instead, the representative person becomes the definition of whatever they represent. That person, and the particular characteristics (or events) connected with that person, which scripture has chosen to accentuate, are forever linked together.

While there are very few such representative people in scriptural history, there are even fewer women. The New Testament gives us an extremely sparse listing of such. This, of course, makes the ones we do find have even greater significance.

Sarah is one of these representative people. As we have seen, she represents holy womanhood and godly feminine beauty. She represents faithfulness to (and respect for) her husband. These qualities, in turn, are inextricably bound up with her renunciation of outward adornment. It's a "package". Each of these factors interrelates with the others, causing them to be seen as they are seen. Their use in connection with Sarah defines them forever. Whatever that definition is - it will be forever. These are the things the Holy Spirit chose to accentuate about Sarah as the representative woman of godly beauty and femininity. Therefore, as far as scripture is concerned, these things (and the attitude of scripture toward them) are forever fixed. How they are presented here will be the standard whereby they are to be judged throughout the ages.

Though we have seen that there are very, very, few biblical representative women, there is at least one more. Her name is Jezebel.

Most certainly, Jezebel is a representative woman. She meets all the qualifications. The New Testament validates this fact by using her as such. She not only dealt Israel a crippling spiritual blow (from which it never fully recovered), but her spirit is seen still doing it's nefarious work in the church age all the way into the book of Revelation - where she causes the church at Thyatira to fall under God's judgment. Thyatira has some commendable points. However, God declares:

> *"Notwithstanding I have a few things against thee, because thou sufferest that woman Jezebel, which calleth herself a prophetess, to teach and to seduce my servants to commit fornication, and to eat things sacrificed unto idols. And I gave her space to repent of her fornication; and she repented not. Behold, I will cast her into a bed, and them that commit adultery with her into great tribulation, except they repent of their deeds... But unto you I say, and unto the rest of Thyatira, as many as have not this doctrine, and which have not known the depths of Satan, as they speak; I will put upon you none other burden" (Rev. 2:20-22,24).*

Here, to be connected with this spirit of Jezebel is equated with "knowing the depths of Satan". This is some of the strongest language of scripture.

Jezebel was a heathen daughter of a heathen priest named Ethbaal. After her marriage to Ahab, king of Israel, she gradually infiltrated Israel with her heathen, Baal-worship religion. Her life eventually became consumed with the challenge of moving Israel away from holiness, and toward heathenistic practices. The religion of Jehovah was a continual rebuke to her spirit. Its holy requirements awakened her hatred of God, and its spiritual worship was intensely offensive and burdensome to her.[17]

Her most hated enemy was the man of God. She used every artifice to seduce God's people into the darkest halls of sin. Through brilliant use of patience and seductive skills, she practically moved God's people down the slippery slide of moral and spiritual depravity single-handedly. She had unusual ability and energy, strong zeal, a superior mind, uncommon astuteness, and great strength of will. Consequently, she left her print in Israel "which no subsequent reformations were able entirely to obliterate".[18]

In stark contrast to Sarah, having a loving, supportive role to her husband was the furthest thing from Jezebel's mind. She was in subjection to neither God nor man. She developed a deep antagonism towards God's prophets which rebuked her depravity, and she worked tirelessly to kill them all, and did cut off many of them (I Kings 18:4). In contrast, she lavishly hosted the prophets of Baal at her table, and regularly funded them (I Kings 18:19). She had Ahab cowed, and the elders of the country were virtually "wrapped around her little finger" (I Kings 21:11). Scripture repeatedly alludes to her whoredoms and also to her witchcraft (II Kings 9:22).

She brooked no opposition by those like Naboth who would not relinquish their inheritance from God so as to please her. His convictions drove her into a frenzy. Where seduction wouldn't work, she resorted to slander, and succeeded in destroying the influence (and lives) of those whose convictions wouldn't allow them to accede to her wishes. Her children were as wild and uncontrolled as their mother, and both boys died prematurely. When one of them sought peace from Jehu, Jehu replied, "...What peace, so long as the whoredoms of thy mother Jezebel and her witchcrafts are so many?" (II Kings 9:22). Jehu then drew a bow "with his full strength, and smote Jehoram between his arms, and the arrow went out at his heart, and he sunk down in his chariot" (9:24).

Only one thing stood between Jezebel and her complete success in seducing the people of God into complete bondage - the man of God, Elijah. In Elijah, God raised up the most powerful prophet in Old Testament history to thwart her deviousness. Only a tireless, courageous, anointed man of God could effectively oppose this seductive spirit. Jezebel, with all of her political, military, and civic power could not defeat this mighty man of God. Thus, Elijah became Jezebel's most bitter enemy. When these two indomitable spirits clashed, the whole country shook, and shock waves reverberated everywhere. The wicked woman, with all the power of the kingdom at her disposal, could not overcome this prophet with "his life of contemplative solitude and extraordinary power for action".[19]

Jezebel's spirit was never broken. She died defiant. On the day Ahab arose early and made his way to possess Naboth's vineyard, two young men rode behind him in his entourage. They were there when Elijah, the prophet, arose like a specter out of the desert to declare in the name of God, "Behold, I will bring evil upon thee..., and will cut off from Ahab every man-child... The dogs shall eat Jezebel by the wall of Jezreel" (I Kings 21:21-23). The young men heard the venerable prophet, and marked his words - for in four more years, Jehu and Bidkar were instrumental in fulfillment of this word.

Jezebel likely knew that the end was near. Her time was short. To meet her fate, she went to her boudoir and calmly made herself up for one last appearance. She painted her eyelashes and eyebrows with antimony, to make the eyes look large and lustrous, and placed her sparkling bejewelled headdress on her head. When her elaborate toilet was completed, she stepped to the palace tower and "looking down through the lattice above the city gate, watched the thundering advance of Jehu's chariot".[20]

Her husband was already dead, and Jehu had become king. She stepped forward in her sensual and alluring disdain. With intense sarcasm (born of deep and incurable bitterness) she calls, "Is it peace, thou Zimri, thou murderer of thy master?". The inference was that Jehu could never succeed because, like Zimri years before him, he had illicitly overthrown his master. The difference was that Jehu had a divine warrant, which Zimri did not have. Jehu shouts up the wall to those who are with Jezebel, "Who is on the Lord's side?". Two servants which recognize Jehu's authority seize her and toss her over the wall. Her body hits the ground, and her blood splashes against the wall. The riders urge their horses forward, and Jezebel is trampled under hooves and wheels. By the time someone comes to bury her, the dogs have beaten them to her, and have consumed her body, leaving nothing except her skull and the bones of her hands and feet. Thus ends the life of Jezebel, but the spirits unleashed by her yet live on.

As we have seen of Sarah and other "representative people", scripture uses them to elucidate a particular truth (or set of truths). This is no less true of Jezebel than of the others. All the things which the Holy Spirit connects with them, and is not modified elsewhere in scripture, is forever defined to reveal God's attitude towards them.

What characterizes Jezebel? Unholiness. Everything about her is unholy. Her spirit is polluted with wickedness, rebellion, and idolatry - which is scripturally defined as spiritual adultery. Her soul is stained with deceit, ruthlessness, and she is the living definition of seduction. Her face is painted, and her body tainted with whoredoms and lasciviousness. Thus, she overwhelmingly towers above all others as the scriptural statement on feminine artificiality and trickery.

We have digressed somewhat from our subject to attempt to provide a broader and deeper understanding of the company that our subject keeps in scripture. It is remarkable how consistent scripture is in portraying face paint and exterior ornamentation in a negative light. Overwhelmingly, its uses in scripture are repeatedly linked with immorality, sensual seduction, brazen shamelessness, unholiness, and disobedience.

For example, Isaiah 3:16-21 gives a detailed list of jewelry worn by the women of Israel, with special attention given to the head and face. Interestingly, God declares, "The shew of their countenance witnesseth against them" (3:9). He further declares that He will take these ornaments (3:18), and shall wash away "...the filth of the daughters of Zion..." (4:4). When this is done, He will replace, and "...will create upon every dwelling place of Mount Zion, and upon her assemblies, a cloud and smoke by day, and the shining of a flaming fire by night: for upon all the glory shall be a defence". Here, again removal of artificiality is connected with the glory of God shining out of the temple. We are the temple of God - may the glory emanate!

The pattern is repeated in Jeremiah. He portrays Israel, in her backslidings, as an adulterous woman, but all of this is recognized in that "...thou clothest thyself with crimson..., thou deckest thee with ornaments of gold..., thou rentest thy face with painting, in vain shall thou make thyself fair; thy lovers will despise thee, they will seek thy life" (Jer. 4:30). Here we see that, just as there is a wisdom of this world that is sensual, earthly, and demonic, so there is a "fairness" that is connected with sensuality, brashness, seduction, and artifice. In contrast, in this same book, God states of His bride: "I have likened the daughter of Zion to a comely and delicate woman" (Jer. 6:2).

Ezekiel makes the same connections.

"And furthermore, that ye have sent for men to come from far, unto whom a messenger was sent; and, lo, they came: for whom thou didst wash thyself, paintedst thy eyes, and deckedst thyself with ornaments. And satest upon a stately bed..." (Ezek. 23:40,41).

This is connected with consorting with "men of the common sort" (v.42), and with adulteries (v.43), lewdness (v.48), and with "defiling my sanctuary" (v.38).

Hosea makes the same connections.

"And I will visit upon her the days of Baalim, wherein she burned incense to them, and she decked herself with her earrings and her jewels, and she went after her lovers, and forgat me, saith the Lord" (Hosea 2:13).

Not only are these connections made in the Old Testament, but also in the New Testament. When John wants to portray the false church, with all of her spiritual seduction and outward allurement, he says: "I saw a woman... arrayed in purple and scarlet color and decked with gold and precious stones and pearls... full of abominations and

125

filthiness of her fornication" (Rev. 17:3,4,). In this same book, when God wanted to describe His people, restored Israel, He uses no such language, but states: "And there appeared... a woman clothed with the sun, and the moon under her feet, and upon her head a crown of twelve stars" (Rev. 12:1). Note that she is "clothed" with (i.e., covered with) the sun! There's no jewelry or face paint mentioned here, but to be "clothed with the sun" does sound like the sparkling, shining, shekinah-glory!

In all of the above, we see cosmetics and jewelry repeatedly linked with unholiness, by both association and direct statements. To the one who decides that these teachings are not for you, that is a prerogative that is certainly available to you. However, for one who is giving a biblical study on these things to declare that scripture does not speak on the subject is to be woefully uninformed, inexcusably negligent, or consciously duplicitous.

I am reminded of a preacher I was listening to (on cassette) sometime ago. In his message, he was discussing these very subjects. He was justifying the use of make-up (by the way, have you ever thought about how much alike the words "make-up" and "make-believe" are? When a child tells an imaginary story, we say he "made-it-up" - it's not the real. When a woman is finished putting on her make-up, it's a "made-up" version of her - it's not the real either. That's kind of a funny thought).

Anyway, this preacher was talking about how, if people didn't believe you ought to use a little paint to make yourself look better, then the next time they buy a car, they should buy one with no chrome, and with no color - just plain black. Thus, they would be consistent. If they bought a house, they needed to buy one with no trim, and only painted some drab color, and so forth.

He meant to be humorous, and he was. The way he said it was funny, and I found myself enjoying a good laugh at the adept way he had presented his point. The more I thought about it, the funnier it got. He was a good speaker, and through use of comparisons he had created an apparent "catch-22" of inconsistency.

Well, the problem was, being as I like a little chrome, I found myself disagreeing with him (although, I did see a woman the other day that appeared to have little chrome strips on her eyes).

Furthermore, I like bright colors. My favorite colors are red and yellow (green is nice too). Therefore that "flat-black" idea didn't set too well either. So what's the options? One option was I could have just said "aw-w-w, he's wrong, just ignore him", but he didn't *sound* wrong - he sounded logical. So I began to think.

I thought... and I thought... and I thought some more. I thought about lots of things. I thought about cars. I thought about houses. I thought about elephants - that's right, elephants. I thought about monkeys, trees, and flowers. I thought about paint.

Somehow, in my mind, "paint" and "elephant" connected. I know it sounds strange, certainly it does. I can't explain it, it just did - "paint - elephant - paint - elephant". It occurred to me that I had never seen a painted elephant. So I imagined someone painting one with a paintbrush, and somehow it just didn't seem right. Oh, it was a very funny sight alright - the paint brush leaving blotchy streaks on the crinkly hide. However, it just wasn't right. It occurred to me that elephants look better natural.

Then, it was the monkeys. You don't have to be an animal-rights activist to know that to paint the monkey isn't right. It just didn't fit. He is as cute as a button in natural tones.

Now I knew that I was on to something! My heart began to race as I thought about roses, ferns, and banana trees (I guess because of the monkeys). I thought about lilies. *None of these are painted*! All of them look much better unpainted and natural. In fact, no amount of paint could match their natural glory, for they were bursting with life from within.

Then I thought about houses again - and cars. Obviously, they need paint - don't look right without it. Then, the difference dawned on me. *These things need paint to have beauty because they are not alive!* Thus, cars need chrome, and houses need trim - but things alive don't need paint, because the life within is the most glorious coloring of all!

So, if you have life within, you don't need paint. If you have no life within, I guess you need paint.

"Consider the lilies of the field, how they grow; they toil not, neither do they spin:And yet I say unto you, That even Solomon in all his glory was not arrayed like one of these" (Matt. 6:28,29).

Dress

Nudist colonies declare that man wasn't made to wear clothes - that clothes are in fact unnatural. They will tell you that man, to be perfectly natural, should not have to wear materials foreign to his/her created state. After all, none of the other animals wear little jackets with ties, or little dresses with pretty bows and high-heel shoes, and they look perfectly fine. Indeed, we don't give it a second thought. No one gets up in the morning and worries what the family dog (or cat) should wear today. They look "complete" with no clothing other than what nature provides. Whether it be in the form of fur, hair, scales, feathers, or whatever, all of them are provided by nature with what they need. So the nudist "buff" says, "Why the fuss about clothes for people? If we had been meant to wear clothes, they would've been provided by nature".

This is not just silliness. This is an important subject. One only has to think of the multi-million dollar clothing industry to realize how basic the subject of clothing is to our humanness. Also, consider how closely tied one's sense-of-self is to how one is dressed. Lastly, we all know that clothing, and how it is used, is a highly sophisticated form of communication to those about us. Clothes talk. How one dresses makes a statement about an individual. This is true whether one is "dressing down", or "dressing up". The whole fashion industry understands and depends upon this fact that "clothes talk". Fashion designers are manipulative experts. Fortunes are spent in the most sophisticated kinds of research to learn and master this art. The populace at large is kept jumping like a puppet on a string, breathlessly rushing from the old to the new, trying to make sure they are "up-to-date". Millions, screaming at the top of their lungs that "I am an individual!", hurry from one magazine to the next making sure they are buying what is fashionably correct so that they can be sure to express their individuality the exact same way that everyone else is expressing theirs. Yes, indeed, clothing plays a very, very, large role among us financially, socially, and psychologically. It also plays a role spiritually.

I agree with the nudists that clothes are not natural. The animals are proof of this point. The life within the animals naturally provides them with a covering. So why should man be different? The answer to this lies above in the first two sentences of this section called "*Dress*". First, we stated that clothes are "unnatural". Second, we stated that man shouldn't have to wear them in his "created state".

The problem is, man is not presently in his "created state". The present state in which we find ourselves is not the created state. This can probably be expressed better by using different terminology.

Man as he was created in the garden (before the fall) was in what is called his "essential" state - that is, he was found there in his undiluted "essence" (from which we get "essential"). After the fall, we find man as he "exists", or in an "existential" state. Obviously, his "existential" state is quite different from his "essential" state, for he has lost the glory, and therefore recognizes himself as being naked. In his "essential" state, man was as God created him - complete, whole, completely alive. As such, we have before stated that there is much evidence that he was not naked at all, but was rather clothed with the glory of God.

One very strong proof of this is that Christ is called "the second man", and "the last Adam" (I Cor. 15:45,47). He is portrayed as having regained the essence for mankind that the first Adam lost through disobedience. In re-attaining this essence, scripture clearly declares that "the glory" (which Adam had lost) is restored to Him (Rev. 5:13). There is no reason to believe that the restored glory appeared any different than the original glory. Thus, repeatedly we see Him whether in His divinity or His victorious human state as being glorious.

"...His countenance was as the sun shineth in his strength" (Rev. 1:16)

"His face did shine as the sun, and His raiment was white as the light" (Mt. 17:2).

"Beloved, now are we the sons of God, and it doth not yet appear what we shall be: but we know that, when He shall appear, we shall be like Him; for we shall see Him as he is" (I Jn. 3:2).

We are not like Him physically yet. Even though our spirits are re-born, and are "like Him", our bodies are still "subject to vanity" (Rom. 8:20), and have not yet been redeemed (Rom. 8:23). Thus, we still catch colds, we grow old, we are attacked by diseases, etc. - and, we still have to wear clothes. However, when we get our new bodies, our clothing will be a new material called "Shekinah". If you are a child of God, you are going to be clothed with this unbelievably white glory-garment!

"And to her was granted that she should be arrayed in fine linen, clean and white: for the fine linen is the righteousness of saints. And the armies which were in heaven followed Him upon white horses, clothed in fine linen, white and clean" (Rev. 19:8,14).

If our fine linen is like His garment (and it is), then this fine linen will be the glory that comes from the righteousness of God, which Adam lost in the garden.

We earlier saw that anything that lives has, as the source of its beauty, the life from God that dwells within it. Things inanimate must have artificial beauty applications from without. At the fall, there is no indication that the animals lost any of their original life - but man did. Something died in Him. God had promised that, "in the day that ye eat thereof, ye shall surely die" (Gen. 2:17). When Adam and Eve ate thereof, they did die - that is their spirits died. Their outward covering had emanated from the life within their spirits. When their spirits died, the glory departed from their spirits, for the glory is always associated with only the living, for it is indeed the source of life. For thousands of years, men lived with their spirits dead to God (i.e., separated from the source of life) - but in Christ, the last Adam, we are "re-born" (or "born again")! Where is this birth? It is in our spirits! That part which died in Adam, and hence in all of us, is "re-born" in the last Adam, and through Him in us! (Acts 13:33; Eph. 2:1). Ye must be born again.

"...Except a man be born...of the Spirit, he cannot enter into the kingdom of God" (Jn. 3:5).

"God is a Spirit, and they who worship Him must worship Him in spirit and in truth" (Jn. 4:24).

Jesus, with anointed incisiveness, described this event of the fall of man in the story of the good Samaritan. It is evident that Jesus intended to teach them this great lesson in this little story. It is interesting to note that he gives prominence in the story to (of all things) clothing!

Five things are mentioned about the traveller in verse 30 of Luke chapter 10.

1. He was on a journey. Life is such a journey.

2. He "fell among thieves". The devil and his hideous minions are the thieves of mankind, robbing man of every good thing.

3. He was "stripped of his raiment". This indicates that, before the fall, man was indeed clothed, but discovers himself naked after the fall. He was stripped of his covering and left exposed. Had he not been stripped, the nudist philosophy would be right (i.e., man doesn't need clothes). However, in his stripped state (and because of it), God provided the temporary bodily covering of clothing until the body is redeemed and "re-clothed" with the glory of God. Thus, the source of clothing is the fall, and every clothing store is a like a trumpet, declaring the fall of man.

4. Man was "wounded". That we now operate short of the potential capacity latent within our humanness is evident everywhere. It is because the race is "wounded", and man's capacity thereby subjected to opposition.

5. The thieves "...departed, leaving him half dead". Man is not fully dead after the fall. His body (and soulish self) lives on,

but that part in which union with God takes place (union with God is another term for "life") has been left destitute. Human history had to await the coming of "the second man" (I Cor. 15:47) to bring a resurrection of the human spirit from the dead back to life.

"And so it is written, The first man Adam was made a living soul; the last Adam was made a quickening {i.e. life-giving} spirit. Howbeit that was not first which is spiritual, but that which is natural; and afterward that which is spiritual. The first man is of the earth, earthy: the second man is the Lord from Heaven. As is the earthy, such are they also that are earthy: and as is the heavenly, such are they also that are heavenly. And as we have borne the image of the earthy, we shall also bear the image of the heavenly" (I Cor. 15:45-49).

Bearing the "image of the heavenly" will be equivalent to being clothed in the glory of God.

The brief thumb-nail sketch above should be carefully understood, for it reveals clearly that the subject of clothing is not only the fabric "on" man, but is connected to the very fabric of what was "in" and was lost, only to be restored in Christ. Clothing is a temporary covering of the body until such time as this body is changed. Even though we are spiritually redeemed, the body is still not so (Rom. 8:23). Unlike the animals, we are not (physically) as we were when we were created. However, the time shall come when "...the dead shall be raised incorruptible, and we shall be changed. For this

135

corruptible must put on incorruption, and this mortal must put on immortality" (I Cor. 15:52,53).

> "For we know that if our earthly house of this tabernacle were dissolved, we have a building of God, and house not made with hands, eternal in the heavens. For in this we groan, earnestly desiring to be clothed upon with our house which is from heaven: If so be that being clothed we shall not be found naked. For we that are in this tabernacle do groan, being burdened not for that we would be unclothed, but clothed upon, that mortality might be swallowed up in life" (II Cor. 5:1-4).

When one looks at the bigger biblical picture of clothing, we are made aware of what a juvenile mistake it would be to get caught up in the transitory fashions of this world. Thus, when God inspired the New Testament writers to admonish believers to dress "in modest apparel", it is not some sadistic attempt on His part to suppress us. Nor is it intended to convey the idea that dress is unimportant. The idea seems to be that, if one ever truly discovers what God is preparing in "His" clothing business, they will then understand how getting caught in this world's fashion is simply out of fashion - "for the fashion of this world passeth away" (I Cor. 7:31). As in the case of other externals for the christian, the attention should be drawn to the glory of the internal and not the sensuousness (or ostentatiousness of the outward). In respect to the human body being the temple of God, the face is the primary window for the shining forth of the glory. Here, the inner person manifests itself, and the beauty of the Lord shines forth. The face of

Moses shining, the face of the Lord shining (Rev. 1:16), scriptural prayers for "the Lord's face to shine upon you" (Num. 6:25), etc., all emphasize this point. The body should be clothed in such a manner and modesty as to lead the eye to the face from whence the glory emanates. Nudity and all sensual dress does just the opposite.

There are other considerations in dress.

Scripture presents a consistent pattern of emphatic insistence concerning distinctions between the sexes. It is equally emphatic regarding these distinctions when it comes to dress. That God regards man and woman as two aspects of a single comprising of His own image is seen in Gen. 1:26,27. To the extent one blurs the distinctions, one removes the manifestation of the divine. Therefore, when artificial means are used to reduce and remove these distinctions, the beginnings of such fashions are invariably from the world which the Bible says to "love not" (I Jn. 2:15).

The biblical directive to maintain these distinctions between men and women is consistent with God's people both in the Old Testament as well as the New Testament. This is true not only of dress, but in many areas which we have seen (i.e., domestic roles, social roles, spiritual roles, as well as spiritual deportment and external symbols of submission to authority). It is important to understand that each of these alone may not seem extremely significant, but scripture portrays each of these as filling a vital role in a bigger framework which even reaches cosmic proportions beyond human understanding (I Cor. 11:10). When one digs deep enough into scriptural teaching regarding humanness, a dawning comes that there is a delicate but very, very real other-worldliness intrinsic to being a human. It is something which living like a beast doesn't eradicate. It is inherent. It is God-like. It is mystical (I use the word carefully). We only see into it obscurely, or "through a glass darkly". The light is dim by which we peer into this hidden mysterious side of our reality. However, it nevertheless is very, very real. Furthermore, it is the part of us that is eternal. It is in this hidden area where the God who hides Himself is found. It is a "secret" area where the "Father which is in secret" is (Mt. 6:6).

When the believing christian comes to this realization, it causes them to give great pause to following leaders who lightly dismiss living life carefully. Following someone who, with considerable disdain, casually relegates life-style questions to the domain of the radical or the ignorant can be a sure ticket to an increasingly empty and shallow existence. Once one has centered their life on trinkets and other trivia for awhile, the serious person will realize the vacuousness of such, and long for the deep probing spiritual flow of divine life. Most assuredly, when the Bible directs us to avoid the world of pretensions and embrace the world of spiritual reality in everyday life, it is directing us to fulfillment and joy.

Thus, for example, a scripture such as Deuteronomy 22:5 takes on additional significance to us.

"The woman shall not wear that which pertaineth unto a man, neither shall a man put on a woman's garment: for all that do so are abomination unto the Lord their God" (Deut. 22:5).

Because this scripture affects everyday life-style, it comes under considerable scrutiny.

In attempting to discount the impact of this scripture for us today, a common position taken is that this scripture is in a setting of many other scriptural instructions to Israel which we do not apply to our lives today, such as putting protective fences on our roofs to prevent injury, sowing a vineyard with different kinds of seeds, etc. The point is often made that since we don't do these other things (many of which would be quite ridiculous and even impossible in our society today), why should we regard 22:5 which deals with distinctions of dress? In answer to this, there are several things to consider.

First, we should consider that Israel was an earthly people with primarily earth-centered promises. Having come out of slavery, and having no concept of even the most basic social and hygiene directives necessary as a responsible people, God provided them with the necessary essentials to create an understanding of the prerequisites for national life. The vast majority of all of the directives in Deuteronomy given in this regard are obviously meant to form a framework for healthy relations between the Israelite and his/her fellowman, as well as his relationship with his animals and his environment. They are given instructions on how to protect their neighbor when he/she comes to their house (22:8), how to protect and nurture the environment (22:6,7), sexual and gender relations (22:13-30), parent-child relations (21:18-23), caring for domestic animals (25:4), etc. There are very, very few directives given that deal with other than relational subjects having to do with Israel and their relationship with their God and their fellowman. For this reason, Jesus summed up the primary teaching of Deuteronomy (and the Law) in Matthew 22:37-40.

> *"...Thou shalt love the Lord thy God with all thy heart, and with all thy soul, and with all thy mind. This is the first and great commandment. And the second is like unto it, Thou shalt love thy neighbour as thyself. On these two commandments hang all the law and the prophets" (Mt. 22:37-40).*

When we read the book of Deuteronomy, we see how true this is. I think most Bible students would agree that this declaration makes clear that the few incidental domestic directives included in Deuteronomy (and they are very few), that do not have a broader relational connection (e.g., "making fringes on the four corners of thy vesture" - 22:12), were not intended to be confused with those issues of broader significance, even though they may appear side by side. However, even these kinds of seemingly innocuous commands were obviously intended to convey, in every way and at every juncture, important general truths of what it meant to be God's people. For example, the making fringes on the four corners of their garments mentioned above was to be a symbolic reminder to Israel to remember God's commands (Num. 15:39). In the same way, the prohibition of sowing different kinds of seeds together (22:9) and the blending of different cloths in a garment were everyday reminders that they were to be a separated, unmixed, unblended people. Their holiness unto the Lord made them His exclusive property, and by virtue of this, they were to be separate and reserved unto God from all others.

However, when we come to verse 5 of chapter 22, there are other factors to consider. One that we have already elaborated upon is that scripture is consistent in insisting on distinctions between the sexes in many areas of life. Another is that, when we carefully ferret out the sources of styles and fashions which create a "unisex" society (both in looks and life-styles), the source is always one which gives no credence to the Bible or regard for pleasing the holy God with a holy life. These alone ought to make the servant of the Lord avoid all such - but there is a more sobering reason. That is, for a woman to wear that which pertaineth to a man, or a man to wear that which pertaineth to a woman is (to use scriptural terminology) "an abomination".

The words "abominable", "abomination", and "abominations" appear 39 times in Leviticus and Deuteronomy, once in Exodus, and none in

Numbers. Of these 39, there are five Hebrew words translated into English as abomination, abominable, or abominations. Four of the five words mean virtually the same thing and share common roots. They mean "disgusting filth, abhorrent". One other word is translated "abominable" and simply means rotten (or fetid) meat (Lev. 19:7), and wasn't used in the context of being abominable to the Lord.

Scripture does not mention many things as being an "abomination to the Lord". In the above-mentioned books, there are only nine things spoken of as being an abomination in the sight of the Lord.

1. Bringing the price of a prostitute or a homosexual prostitute into the house of the Lord to pay a pledge (Deut. 23:18).

2. Homosexuality (Lev.18:22).

3. Idolatry, including sacrificing children to walk in the fire (Deut. 18:9,10, 20:18 and many other references).

4. The occult (Deut. 18:10-12).

5. A woman wearing that which pertaineth to a man, or a man wearing that which pertaineth to a woman (Deut. 22:5).

6. Using unjust measuring devices to cheat (Deut. 25:13-16).

7. A husband divorcing a woman, then remarrying her after she had been married to another in between times (Deut. 24:1-4).

8. Offering blemished sacrifices to God (Deut. 17:1).

9. Eating unclean animals (Deut. 14:3). (This one is clearly changed in Acts 10:11-16).

It is evident from the above list that violation of Deut. 22:5 casts us into very unsavory company. Sodomites, prostitutes, pimping money, twisted marital relations, idolatry, child abuse, cheaters, and tainted offerings - that's not good company for a child of God. It is the company in which violators of Deut. 22:5 find themselves.

There are many other prohibitions, directives, commands, etc., given in the Law as recorded in Exodus, Leviticus, Numbers, and Deuteronomy. However, only the eight above (minus #9 which the New Testament itself erases) qualify as an abomination - that is being disgustingly abhorrent in the eyes of the Lord. The question is, if the other seven are obviously still wrong, the prohibition's still in effect for today, and still qualify as abominable in the sight of the Lord, then how is it suddenly logical to expect #5 (listed above) to be any different than the others? Thus, to attempt to disqualify Deut. 22:5 on the basis that there are other prohibitions in Deuteronomy that we do not heed is not sound reasoning, for these other things do not come under the over-arching umbrella of being an "abomination to the Lord". Incidentals were never listed as abominations. Anything which qualified as an abomination under the Law in Deuteronomy, and not explicitly removed in the New Testament, remains an abomination now.

Others who have attempted to negate Deut. 22:5 have proposed the idea that the Hebrew word which was translated "man" in Deut.22:5, should actually be translated "soldier". This is based upon the fact that the word "man" used here comes from a root meaning "strong". However, we should be careful here not to automatically connect "strong" to the idea of a soldier only, for this also applies to masculinity and the biblical definition of manhood. That the word here translated "man" is not translated "soldier" in our English version (not even once) seems strange, if the above is true, especially when it is translated "man" at least 48 times throughout the Old Testament! We have seen that the actual origin of the word comes from the meaning "to be strong", and originally meant a valiant, or strong man. However, that it came to mean simply man, and was a synonym for other words which meant "man", is clearly obvious from its Old Testament usage elsewhere. For example, Prov. 30:19 speaks of "the way of a man with a maid". The word "man" is the same as is used in Deut. 22:5, and obviously should be translated as it is, rather than "warrior", or "soldier". Psa. 34:8 (speaking of the Lord) says, "Blessed is the man that trusteth in Him". Again, this is the same word as in

Deut. 22:5. Once again, it is obvious that it is correctly translated (for other examples, see Psa. 18:25, 37:23, 40:4, 127:5, etc.).

The Hebrew And English Lexicon Of The Old Testament, by Brown, Driver, and Briggs (which, I suppose, is as authoritative as it is possible to get) defines this Hebrew word "geber" (which is translated "man" in English in Deut. 22:5) as simply "man", and goes on to explain that it means "man as strong, distinguished from women, children, and non-combatants whom he is to defend". They also point out that this "strong" idea is chiefly poetic, and cite examples of the same. It is man as "strong" as compared to women and children, not man "strong" as a soldier compared to other men.[21] A number of resources make the observation that not only does Deut. 22:5 address the issue of dress, but it includes the extended idea of a man's implements (i.e., masculine things that obviously are "man things". Of this, Keil-Delitzch, in their highly respected Commentary on the Old Testament, make the following observation:

> Deut. 22:5: "As the property of a neighbour was to be sacred in the estimation of an Israelite, so also the divine distinction of the sexes, which was kept sacred in civil life by the clothing peculiar to each sex, was to be not less but even more sacredly observed. The wording does not signify clothing merely, nor arms only,

but includes every kind of domestic and other utensils (as in Ex. 22:6; Lev. 11:32, 13:49). The immediate design of this prohibition was not to prevent licentiousness, or to oppose idolatrous practices (the proofs which Spencer has adduced of the existence of such usages among heathen nations are very far-fetched); but maintain the sanctity of that distinction of the sexes which was established by the creation of man and woman, and in relation to which Israel was not to sin. Every violation (or wiping out) of this distinction (i.e., emancipation of a woman) was unnatural, and therefore an abomination in the sight of God".[22]

The above not only makes it clear that the verse includes a man's "things" in its prohibition, but also makes clear that the verse is not referring to some supposed heathen rites which Israel would be tempted to emulate. More evidence that this verse should not be narrowly understood to apply to some connection to heathen rites, but rather has a broad and general ethical application, is further seen in the following:

"The divinely instituted distinction between the sexes

was to be sacredly observed, and in order to this, the dress and other things appropriate to the one were not to be used by the other - 'That which pertaineth to a man' (literally, the apparatus of a man, not merely dress, but implements, tools, weapons and utensils). This is an ethical regulation in the interests of morality. There is no reference, as some have supposed, to the wearing of masks for the purpose of disguise, or to the practice of the priests (at heathen festivals) wearing masks of their gods. Whatever tends to obliterate the distinction between the sexes tends to licentiousness; and that the one sex should assume the dress of the other has always been regarded as unnatural and indecent".[23]

In regards to whether men and women could do certain activities better if allowed to wear the attire of the other, perhaps someone said it best in stating "Whatever forbids my robe, forbids my presence".[24] Utilitarian considerations are never given preference over holiness considerations in scripture.

So just what is men's apparel and women's apparel? The answer to this question is not complicated. Biblical society (and virtually every other society) has always had feminine and masculine distinctions in dress. Historically, men and women have worn robes of one kind or another for almost all of human history. The robe has been the accepted form of dress for rich and poor, for ruler and ruled, for men and for women. Thus, the distinctiveness of masculine and feminine attire was reduced to distinguishing markings, cuts, and lengths, as well as having to do with the degree of delicateness, daintiness, and fineness of texture. This is well-documented in history, and is hardly subject to question.

The other major distinction in dress between men and women was not simply what they wore but how they wore it. There were "man ways" of utilizing the robe for dress that were distinctive to maleness, just as their were feminine distinctives exclusive to femininity.

By virtue of being a man (and thus physically stronger), the man was the one primarily responsible for provision and protection of his family. He engaged in masculine activities that the women were not required to do, and in fact were instructed not to do. These were things that had to do with physical exertion and activity which required a high degree of movement. Included in this were activities such as vigorously tilling the fields, hurriedly travelling over dangerous roads in the pursuit of business responsibilities, and/or military duties, and preparing for battle. In order to be effective in these (and other areas like them),

148

men had to find ways to deal with their clothing in such a way as to keep it from tripping them, or hindering their dexterity of movement. Their business successes, and sometimes their very lives depended upon suitable solutions in dealing with the cumbersomeness of their robes. To manage their robes in such a way that their movements would be unimpeded, they devised a system of folds and tucks which transformed the robe into a snug-fitting, flexible garment. From this came the practice known as "girding up their loins". Women had ways of girding themselves. However, when a man girded himself, it was a way distinctive to men. A woman would never so gird herself, for it would have been considered grossly immodest. The strong, active man, to avoid getting entangled in his garment, would reach down and pull his robe up tucking all of this lower material into his waistband. This drew the robe up against his body, creating a snug-fitting kind of trouser-like effect. With the robe so tucked, it provided him with the freedom of movement necessary for strong physical exertions. This devising was in alignment with his manly responsibilities. In conjunction with this, when God wanted Job to stand up and take his manly accountability, he commanded him to "Gird up now thy loins *like a man*; for I will demand of thee, and answer thou me" (Job 38:3). While God here demanded Job to gird up his loins "like a man", nowhere does scripture so instruct a woman - for such girding was inappropriate for a woman. This girding created a somewhat form-fitting effect and was a distinctively masculine thing to free him to do his duties. Peter later uses this analogically when he instructs: "Wherefore gird up the loins of your mind, be sober..." (I Pet. 1:13). Of this verse, Charles Ryrie, in the footnotes of the Ryrie Study Bible, states: "A figure of speech based on the gathering and fastening up of the long, eastern garments so that they would not interfere with the individual's activity". The idea here again is for the mind (like men's girded bodies) to be so freed from encumbrance as to be able to act quickly and decisively. "With the long, loose robes which were commonly worn in the east, a girdle was very necessary when a man wished to do any active work. When men were at ease, their robes fell loosely around them, but the first thing in preparing for walking (or for work) was to tighten the girdle and tuck up the long skirts of the robe."[25]

"The figure is oriental. The orientals wore a loose and flowing robe, which dangling about the feet hindered swift straight motion. When they would move quickly and with precision, they must needs gather the trailing garment into the girdle about the waist".[26]

Historically, the fact that the first men's trousers were "knee-britches" may be connected to the actuality that this is approximately where a girded robe struck the leg as it was pulled upward and tucked in the front waist band. This may be why pants have historically been men's apparel - not only in secular history, but (in this sense) in biblical history as well. It is remarkable that when God demanded that Job face Him in a masculine posture of accountability, He did so by addressing the state of his robe! The masculine action of girding up his loins in man-like fashion became God's symbol of his manhood and his acceptance of manly responsibilities. Perhaps, we do this too (in a way) when we ask, "Who wears the pants in this family?".

From the above, it seems there is little question of what is and isn't "man's apparel". These distinctions do not go unnoticed in the world. It is ironic that just last week the news reported that a lesbian is bringing formal protest against the use of the present male/female symbols on public rest rooms. This is being done on the basis that it discriminates between the sexes by picturing one in trousers and the other in a dress. She wants this distinction removed. David Bernard points out that feminist Susan Brownmiller, as part of her revolt against God-given distinction between male and female, stopped wearing dresses and skirts altogether.[27] In her protest of "imposed limitations" of femininity, she is victimized by the imposed limitations of rebellion!

To the author's knowledge, there is no society or culture in recorded human history where trousers were the natural, normal dress for women. If one wants to say it doesn't matter, they may do so. However, to propose the idea that trousers are not men's apparel, but women's apparel, is farfetched.

To reiterate what was earlier stated, our purposes for going this deeply into these areas of scripture, and their resulting ethical implications, is because there are many who want to know more about these things. There is a deep and keen interest in life-style issues. Increasingly in our society, there are fewer and fewer cultural norms to give guidance. That there is a marked and very recognizable destabilization of historically accepted values is easy for any observant person to see. When a society's mores and values are shaped by forces which are hedonistic and godless, the godly must be committed to biblical values and spiritual realities. On the other hand, those who are overly concerned of what non-christians think of them become increasingly world-and-acceptance conscious. As for me, I can testify that I have no interest in being re-enslaved by anything that leads towards the insatiable appetites of the flesh. Some of those who talk most about bondage have been raised in a "hot-house" of christian protectionism, and don't know what real bondage is. Like the "goofy goose", they waddle into each new wind of doctrine unaware of the vicious and insidious forces that lie in wait to rend them. Their children often pay an even greater price. Unfortunately, they do not realize that what they think of as an emancipating lark is, in fact, the beginning of a long, long walk down a steeply declining path - the end of which is a pernicious bondage in a place of unspeakable darkness.

*"But there were false prophets also among the people, even as there shall be false teachers among you, who privily shall bring in damnable heresies, even denying the Lord that bought them, and bring upon themselves swift destruction. **And many shall follow their pernicious ways; by reason of whom the way of truth shall be evil spoken of...** For when they speak great swelling words of vanity, they allure through the lusts of*

the flesh, through much wantonness, those that were clean escaped from them who live in error. **While they promise them liberty, they themselves are the servants of corruption: for of whom a man is overcome of the same is he brought in bondage. For if after they have escaped the pollutions of the world through the knowledge of the Lord and Saviour Jesus Christ, they are again entangled therein, and overcome, the latter end is worse with them than the beginning. For it had been better for them not to have known the way of righteousness, than, after they have known it, to turn from the holy commandment delivered unto them.** *But it is happened unto them according to the true proverb, The dog is turned to his own vomit again; and the sow that was washed to her wallowing in the mire"* (II Pet. 2:1,2,18-22).

In contrast, the clean, powerful, love-filled world of God's presence holds the promise of one's becoming the full person God intended each of us to be. In this process, some things are obviously of greater weight than others. However, all of God's ways, including life-style issues, build us upon Jesus Christ.

"In whom all the building fitly framed together groweth unto an holy temple in the Lord: In whom ye also are builded together for an habitation of God through the Spirit" (Eph. 2:21,22).

Chapter 9

Veil Of Glory

In I Corinthians 11:1-16, we find another area where men and women have two differing ways of physically exemplifying the glory of God. We have already observed that God made mankind in His image - as male and female, so they could more completely reveal God in their respective, distinctive characteristics. In this case, the characteristic of the man is to be that the hair of his head is shorn. In contrast, the distinctiveness of the woman is her long, unshorn hair.

> *"...if a woman have long hair, it is a glory to her: for her hair is given her for a covering" (I Cor. 11:15).*

Not only does Paul teach that "her hair is given her for a covering", but he states of the man, "...a man indeed ought not to cover his head".

> "...if a man have long hair, it is a shame unto him" (11:14).

The task of determining "what is long hair" in this passage is a simple one. Length of hair is described in only three ways - "long" (vs. 14,15), "shorn" (v. 6), and "shaven" (v. 6). "Shorn" means "to shear, or cut", regardless of length. "Shaven" of course means to cut off completely - as when a man shaves his face with a razor. Obviously, it is not the same as "shorn", or there would be no need for Paul to use two words instead of one. "Long", the definition of which is done for us by scripture - in that it uses it in conjunction with "shaven" and "shorn", which eliminates any definition other than uncut.

Interestingly, a man's cut hair and a woman's long (uncut) hair are both linked (by scripture) with the "glory" of God. Once again, we see the believer's body as the temple of God, which is to be aligned with God's wishes - so as to manifest the shekinah-glory of God.

Paul states that the christian woman's hair is her "covering". Prior to Paul's writings, a woman's covering was a cloth veil. All women wore veils, and to go unveiled was a sure sign of a bold woman of loose morals. The idea of the veil was that a woman "hid" her beauty from the eyes of others, and reserved it for her husband at home (this idea was also revealed in the clothing - in Bible times, women wore dark, plain colors in public, and reserved their bright attraction-getting clothes for the privacy of their homes for the benefit and pleasure of their husbands). Thus, Paul teaches that the woman is to be covered, because she is (i.e., her glory is) the glory of the man (v.7). The man, on the other hand, is the image and glory of God (who is everywhere in the open). Therefore man's shorn hair is the equivalent of giving his glory to God openly.

Because Paul's instruction regarding the woman having long hair becomes a daily physical reality (thus creating a distinctive), there are those who, for whatever reason, declare that this teaching is not relevant to us today and is therefore non-binding. This is done on the basis of a number of purported reasons - not the least of which is the proposal that this was only a cultural teaching of Paul, and therefore was never intended to have ongoing authority. Some also teach that this was a particular proposal for only Corinth, due to particular problems associated with Corinth exclusively.

Once again we want to remind our readers that, while institutional christianity (as well as many other groups) has attempted coercion throughout history, Christ did not. He leads - He never drives. Pure elemental christianity is only for those who accept an invitation, not a demand. However, one should always keep in mind, when scripture speaks to us on any subject, disobedience to that instruction always brings in its wake a whole package of undesirable side effects - many of which are not apparent until it is too late. Scripture gives us many, many examples of things in the visible being vitally connected with breath-taking things in the universal invisible. For example, Job evidently had no idea that the whole universe was watching his little drama unfold. Every detail of his life became scrutinized, and little did he realize that he was on the largest stage ever known to man. Maybe Paul was in this frame of mind when he declares that the christian woman, in reference to her long hair, should have "power on her head because of the angels" (I Cor. 11:10). I believe this scripture (and all scripture) is applicable to us today.

To start down the road of picking and choosing what applies to us, and what does not, is certainly a mine field of dangerous possibilities. People have historically done this with scores of different Bible teachings - casting aside what doesn't fit their plan and idea, and taking license to live in disregard to scriptural teaching on the matter. Of course, this never leads to greater blessing, but rather to a growing disregard for clear statements of scripture.

Let's look at the dilemmas that are created by citing actual examples of the practice of deciding some scriptures do not apply to us.

First of all, Acts 2:38 was spoken to Jews. Therefore, it is taught by some that the promise of the Holy Ghost is not for us - for this only applied to that particular group for that particular time. Of course, for those of us who have received the Holy

Ghost, we know this is not true - for we have received it! An argument is seldom, if ever, as powerful as an encounter! Nevertheless, this does not prevent some from making the above assertion.

Further there are non-spirit-filled Bible scholars who do not believe one should derive doctrine from any of the book of Acts because it is historical and not "didactic". Therefore, according to them, we now need to re-examine whether Acts, and its examples, even apply to us today in a doctrinal way. This teaching has become particularly "in vogue" recently. It is a flimsy excuse to try to avoid teachings on the baptism of the Holy Ghost, and is completely driven back into silence (where it belongs) by author Roger Stronstad in a book every Pentecostal preacher should have - The Charismatic Theology Of St. Luke". Furthermore, Paul declares: "All scripture is given by inspiration of God, and is profitable *for doctrine... for instruction...*" (II Tim. 3:16). "All" includes the book of Acts.

Others believe Matthew is written for the Jews only - with others believing it was written only to the Gentiles. Still others teach that the whole idea of Spirit-infilling (with speaking in tongues) was for a specific place and time, to accomplish certain things which were intertwined with the Jewish people's spiritual and cultural milieu, and that none of it is for us (of course, anyone who has lived in the Master's house and nation, knows He has given His own speech to communicate with Him! - I Cor. 14:2).

We can go on and on. For example, Moses didn't write the first five books of the Bible, some say. Isaiah didn't write all of Isaiah, others say. Eventually, by listening to a hundred different voices instead of the "written voice of God", there's little or nothing left, because *we* decided that what's there doesn't apply to us, that it's spurious, or it doesn't mean what it says.

So what happens? We become like Thomas Jefferson who liked and believed certain parts of the New Testament, but didn't believe other parts, so he compiled his own version of the Bible - inserting what he wanted and deleting what didn't suit his fancy.

All of this basically ties in with the fact that, the combative servant always demanding legal language will seek out what he/she perceives to be "the minimums" that can be "gotten away" with. The love-slave, on the other hand, would be horrified at the thought of bringing shame to her Master, or Head (I Cor. 11:5,7). Whether or not she could "get away with it" is not even a consideration. She never considers the question, "will disobedience ban me eternally from the Master's house?". Why is this so? Because love seeks to please its object - not itself. It "seeketh not its own". The Master's pleasure is her pleasure. True love doesn't entangle itself with legal questions regarding minimums. In contrast, true love always seeks to maximize the degree of its commitment.

So what happens when we begin to decide that some clear New Testament teachings are for us, while others are cultural? Could we find ourselves unwittingly sitting in the seat of God, and in effect rewriting portions of the Bible? If parts of the New Testament were meant for then and not now, who is to determine this, and by what authority? If one has the power to delete I Cor. 11:1-16, does another have authority to delete the book of Acts (including all of its spiritual experiences)?

Earlier, I mentioned claims made against the book of Isaiah, the Pentateuch, the book of Matthew, the book of Acts, etc. All of these claims are real claims. I did not make them up. They can be easily documented - and that's just the tip of the iceberg. There are hundreds of such claims, coming from all directions. I would think we would all want to avoid being included in such company - for it is a crowd with "many kinds of voices", and trumpets with "uncertain sounds".

So what should we believe? We should believe the Bible. It is God's Word. The New Testament is the new covenant. It is a unilateral contractual agreement, based on love, between God and His people. As we have seen, a covenant of this nature, once entered into with God, was forever.

Such covenants had their clear instructions, and had their visible symbols which signified their submission to the stipulations of the agreement. These symbols were so closely intertwined with the covenant itself that to destroy the symbol was, in many cases, to destroy the covenant. Thus, when Samson's symbol was cut off, his power was cut off also. From Samson, we see that, when one has real inward power (the glory) which has been connected by God to outward symbols of this covenant relationship, to destroy the outward is to begin the process of dismantling the inward. In the case of the christian woman who loves the Master's house, her symbol of submission to covenant with her head (i.e., her husband, Christ, and God - I Cor. 11:3) was her long hair, which we have already seen is defined by its usage as uncut hair. Her power, like Samson's in his nazarite vow, is linked with its symbol.

> *"For this cause ought the woman to have power on her head..." (I Cor. 11:10).*

There will always be those who "pick and choose" what parts of the covenant they will accept. For example, in I Corinthians 12, Paul gives explicit teaching about the gifts of the Spirit. However, there are those who say that the gifts of the Spirit are not for us. They say, "that is not for us - that was just for those days".

In chapter 14, Paul gives instruction on how to have order in a church service and still have the working of the Spirit. Of this, others say, "That was just for that day. That is not applicable to us today".

In chapter 9, Paul teaches, "they that preach the gospel should live of the gospel", and to "muzzle not the ox that treadeth out the corn". Again, there are those today who say, "we have a better system. That was fine for Paul's day, but not us. We have more sophisticated systems". However, that does not change the Word of God.

In chapter 11, Paul states, "Doth not even nature itself teach you, that, if a man have long hair, it is a shame unto him. But if a woman have long hair, it is a glory to her for her hair is given her for a covering" (vs. 14,15). He also teaches that for her to be shorn is to be unveiled (or uncovered) - and that this is shameful (v. 6). Paul saw this outward distinction between men and women as being rooted deep in the very ground of creation and natural order (vs. 7-9,14).

Once again, we remind the reader that we are simply reiterating Paul's teaching. There are numerous Bible scholars who quite openly disagree with him. You, the reader, may do so also. However, for me, that is not a reasonable option. For, I believe the Bible is the inspired Word of God. I believe that Paul, as well as the rest of the writers of the Bible, wrote as they were led and moved on by the Holy Spirit. I also believe that their writings have authority that neither mine, nor anyone else's, has. I believe we can write things that are just as Spirit-anointed as their's was. However, if we write (or espouse anything) that disagrees with the "forever settled" writings of scripture, there can be no question of which is right - the Bible is. Even if we fast 40 days, and an angel (or new "prophet") gives us "new light" which purportedly offsets scripture, or supersedes scripture, the old scripture is still right. The prophet thundered: "remove not the ancient landmarks". If lightning accompanies the "new word", and if the most "enlightened" of men declare it to be true, it's still false - for God doesn't establish His guidelines according to the latest popularity poll, nor does He seem to be concerned when the heathen rage. If one wants to go somewhere besides heaven (which is the Master's ultimate "house", Jn. 14:1-3), or wants to be with someone besides the holy Jesus (who is both first and last, and who created all things, and by Him all things consist - Col. 1:15-18), then I would suggest to do whatever you "feel" is right. Follow your logic. Use your rational mind. Make your own decisions. However, if your first and foremost concern is the Master, then follow His Word and rejoice in your salvation!

So we ask ourselves, did Paul himself see his teachings in I Corinthians as being for everyone, or just for Corinth? Did he expect others than the Corinthian church to pick through his teachings and eliminate those things they didn't care for? Or, did he expect his teachings to be universal and applicable to every church everywhere?

One certainly doesn't have to be a Bible scholar to see that Paul taught the same things everywhere he went. He had standardized guidelines and instruction, and he did intend for it to be for every believer everywhere. Ironically, it is in the book of I Corinthians that he emphasizes this the most.

"Unto the church of God which is at Corinth, to them that are sanctified in Christ Jesus, called to be saints, with all that in every place call upon the

name of Jesus Christ our Lord, both their's and our's" (I Cor. 1:2).

It also becomes obvious that Paul was consistent in his teachings to all the churches. For example, when dealing with marriage questions (Chapter 7), Paul gives instruction, then as a validation for the authority of his teaching, he declares: "...so ordain I in all churches" (7:17).

Again, in chapter 4, when Paul's authority is questioned, he informs them that he is sending Timothy to them.

"...who shall bring you into remembrance of my ways which be in Christ, as I teach everywhere in every church" (4:17).

Again, in chapter 11, Paul is dealing with those outward forms of submission (i.e., of the man being "unveiled" by having cut hair, and the woman being "veiled" by her long - uncut hair). In his teaching on this, Paul takes into account that there may be some who would disagree with him, or who may accuse him of attempting to make Corinth do something that was not a standard of the other churches. To counteract this potential charge, Paul plainly explains to them: "Now if anyone is disposed to be argumentative and contentious about this, we hold to and recognize no other custom {in worship} than this, nor do the churches of God generally" (I Cor. 11:16, Amplified version). Here again, we see yet another, clear example that Paul's teachings on all these subjects were not exclusively to Corinth (nor only to his time), but that he was consistent in teaching the same in all churches, and his teaching had final authority.

For us to decide whether Paul's teachings are for us today, we must determine whether or not he had both the authority and the intent for them to be universally applicable. That he had the intent for them to be universally applicable is obvious from the numerous examples already cited.

In regards to the question of Paul's authority, as the apostle to the Gentiles and writer of much of the New Testament, he assumes an enormous amount of authority, and doesn't hesitate to use any source at his disposal to reinforce his teaching on a given subject. For example, in I Cor. 4:17, he teaches them on no stronger basis than "...my ways which be in Christ", and reinforced it with a warning based on nothing more than his personal power with (and anointing from) God. Again, in his instruction on marriage in chapter 7, he puts the final stamp of authority on it by simply saying, "And so ordain I in all churches".

In chapter 9, he reinforces his insistence on the material support of the ministry by pulling an obscure passage about oxen out of the Old Testament, and uses it as a reinforcement for his teaching (9:6). In the entire Bible, no one ever gave such an audacious interpretation to such an innocuous scripture! Yet, the Holy Spirit, through Paul, takes this little "farm animal" passage, and pumps it full of important truth for the church (this shows us also that Old Testament scriptures can apply to the New Testament in several different ways). One is by direct and straightforward application of what is actually said (Deut. 22:5). Another is by extrapolating, out of a domestic scripture, a typological meaning which is not directly stated in the scripture, but is drawn out of it by the use of parallels. A perfect example of this is seen in Paul's use of the ox treading out the corn. In Deut. 25:4, we have an example of an extrapolation of a meaning out of a scripture that is not actually stated, but is there typologically, waiting to be lifted out by the all-knowing knowledge of the Holy Spirit.

When we see how the Holy Spirit does this occasionally in the New Testament, it makes us very cautious about discounting any Old Testament scripture as not containing potential content which is applicable to us today. It is my opinion that, in eternity, we will be absolutely flabbergasted at how many things were hidden in scripture which none of us ever discovered.

In chapter 11, in his discussion of submission to authority, Paul does no differently here than in the other chapters. He is consistent throughout the book in his approach to establishing foundational, ethical, moral guidelines, and the outworking of these in everyday life. As he does in the other chapters, he uses every available resource to drive home his God-given directives for the church.

In chapter 11 he is dealing with the man's hair being shorn and the woman's being the opposite (long/unshorn and unshaven), as a natural sign of submission to their respective authority. To make the strongest case possible, Paul follows his usual pattern of appealing to every possible area to strengthen his doctrinal position. In this case, he appeals to at least five things to establish his premise that men's submission to their head is symbolized by shorn hair, and the women's by long/unshorn hair.

- He appeals to divine order of authority (v. 3).

- He appeals to creation (vs. 7-9).

- He appeals to natural order (vs. 14,15).

- He appeals to their custom (v. 6).

- He appeals to the example of the other churches (v. 16).

Carefully and methodically, Paul brings each of these witnesses to the stand to testify that his teaching, regarding submission and its outward symbols, is correct.

Paul's first concern seemed to be that they would understand that the already established practice of women being veiled and men unveiled was correct. Its significance was validated by the fact that it was anchored in the very nature of creation, and should thus be continued. However, as was his way, Paul takes this to new ground with a bold assertion that they were to understand that a woman's hair was given for her covering (v. 15). Before that, a cloth veil covered her, but Paul now asserts that her long, unshorn hair of her head outwardly signifies her submission to her head (i.e., her husband and Christ).

That Paul should here take it upon himself to take old truths to new (and heretofore uncharted) levels should not surprise us. When we look at the way he unpacks new truths on other New Testament subjects, he is quite consistent in his approach. His boldness in deriving new foundational precepts from old accepted truths reveals in him a confidence that he is ordained of God to lay this new foundation. That he did indeed have this authority is readily evident by (a) his position of prominence in scripture as the apostle to the Gentiles; (b) the fact that he alone was the first to see the church in its true perspective (Eph. 1:9,10); and (c) the fact of his authorship of the majority of the New Testament. Understanding this helps us to see why Paul could speak of "...my ways" (4:17) as being authoritative, or freely state "so ordain I in all churches" (7:17). It also shows more clearly why he declares his Corinthian teachings to also be applicable to "...all that in every place call upon the name of Jesus Christ our Lord, both theirs and ours" (1:2).

Another interesting Pauline trait is his habit of tying a seemingly insignificant thing (like shorn hair) to much larger, universal truths, which are themselves pregnant with far greater importance and significance. Another way of saying this is that whatever Paul recognized as important, he formed

169

a theology for it and anchored it therein. He seldom, if ever, leaves any of his teachings on specific codes of conduct to stand alone. He invariably sets them in a theological framework of greater, broader truths. By doing so, he greatly increases the significance of that which may seem unimportant at first glance. From this, we see once more that trivializing anything in God's Word is something which the wise steward avoids.

I Corinthians 11:1-16 is a good example of how Paul "theologizes" various features of a given subject, and thereby imbues its various disparate parts with previously unmerited importance. What was heretofore only a custom is poured full of new meaning, and (in its new form) established as a New Testament standard. He takes the issue of veiling to new heights unheard of. He attaches ethical significance to this now-elevated custom. He marshals twice the amount of witnesses he needs to corroborate his position. As we have seen, in the space of 16 verses, he appeals to divine order (v. 3), creation (vs. 7-9), nature (vs. 14,15), custom (v. 6,16), and the example of the other churches (v. 16). In addition, he appeals to their own good judgment (v. 13) and to his own judgment (vs. 4,5). He even throws in a few "cosmic reasons" for maintaining this standard, by expressing that even the angels are affected by this (v. 10). Thus, we have seven witnesses called by Paul to support his position that the christian male's shorn hair and the christian woman's unshorn hair are important symbols linked forever as outward manifestations of inward submission to being vessels which exude God's glory.

170

Paul's habit of seeing what appears to be "small things" in a larger context is important. It is difficult, if not impossible, to find examples of Paul discussing seemingly small things apart from their connections to larger truths. For him, it is not a question of "can we lop this off and still survive", or "can we do without that". He does not attempt to dissect and leave small pieces of disparate theological parts lying everywhere. Rather, he envisions a building "fitly framed" and sees all aspects of this teaching as necessary to the development of an integrated, healthy christianity. He, in effect, teaches us that even if we do not see in every case, the integrated significance of every part, its significance is there, and his teaching should therefore be heeded.

The interesting thing about this particular passage we have been discussing (I Cor. 11:1-16) is that upon close inspection, it becomes obvious that these Corinthian christian women were taking their new-found freedom in christianity too far. They saw open to them new opportunities which they had never before been allowed. They were praying in public worship and prophesying. They were evidently doing significant ministry which Paul acknowledges. With this, it appears that under the intoxication of their new-found joy and freedom in Christ, they were in danger of going too far. In their recognition that in Christ, there is neither male nor female, their logic was that "if we now have these other freedoms (i.e., praying and prophesying), then let's also remove other eradicable distinctions between male and female - such as elimination of the veil".

Paul's answer to this is basically one of agreement that, yes, in the spirit, any distinctions of spiritual power have indeed been erased. However, he goes on to show that even though the above is true in the spirit, we nevertheless remain in our created state as man and woman, and there still remains valid and unchanged natural distinctions. Furthermore, he evidently is willing to concede to the removal of the man-made veil, but only because nature has its own veil (i.e., hair - v.15).

Paul here teaches that the nature of man and woman and their respective roles makes some things inviolate, even in the face of the Corinthian christians' real, new spiritual freedom. Secondly, he also teaches that spiritual freedom does not change creation's distinctions between the man and the woman. Spiritual revival restores a man to full "manness" and woman to full "womanness", but does not "de-gender" them.

As we have already seen, there is a reason that mankind is created as man and woman rather than simply as one or the other. The idea is that mankind is created in the image of God. By looking at mankind, a reflection (however dim) of what God is can be seen. This view is incomplete unless seen from both sides of mankind. To fulfill there respective roles with all their potential is also the way to personal fulfillment by either male or female. When the distinction is removed, or ignored, the purpose of mankind's existence (that is to find complete wholeness and fulness as a human, and to thereby reveal God) is eroded, and the purposes of God thus thwarted. The above is a primary element in the Bible's consistent and unbending insistence on emphasizing the distinctions of male and female. Everywhere we look, we see this truth driven home. In dress (Deut. 22:5), Spirit (I Pet 3:5), hair (I Cor 11:15), roles (Eph. 5:23-28), and authority (I. Cor. 11:7-9), the Bible relentlessly presses home the critical nature of these distinctions. With this in mind, it doesn't seem strange that a hedonistic and humanistic society should always be moving toward a unisex, anti-God, mind-set. It does seem strangely convoluted reasoning when christian leaders spend time and expense to encourage a destruction of such distinctions among christian believers. While acknowledging every man's God-given responsibility to work out his own salvation, we nevertheless believe it appropriate at this time to issue a sober word of caution to believers tempted to follow the opinions of men who would presume to "interpret away" the clear teachings of the most foremost apostles and writers of the New Testament - namely, Paul and Peter. When one considers that the New Testament is no bigger than it is, but that God nevertheless considers such things important enough to deal with in considerable detail, extreme care should be taken before deciding to simply disregard such teaching. As limited in size as it (the New Testament) is, it really seems strange to further reduce it by arbitrarily deciding that sizable chunks of it do not apply to us today and can be simply disregarded. That kind of foundation seems "very sandy". Matthew 7:26 gives a very harsh definition of the kind of people who build on sand.

Chapter 10

Grace The Source, Love The Reason

Finally, we have come to the point where one asks, "Is obedience to what we have learned necessary?". Are these things, along with other claims of Christ on our lives, things which we should take seriously?

The answer is, of course, yes. That is, if one understands and is concerned about having one's life aligned as completely as possible with the arrangements which are laid down biblically, and if one believes that biblical principles are normative for christian everyday living. However, there are two more things which we should consider.

Grace The Source

The source of obedience of the true christian is grace. We recognize God's claim on our lives because our God is "the God who is gracious to us in Jesus Christ".[28] Our obedience to God is inextricably bound up with our reception of divine grace in and following conversion.[29] In Paul's teachings, the basis of obligation is that the christian "is" the pure, unleavened, temple of God, therefore we are to "be" what we "are" (I Cor. 5:7).

To categorize obedience as "works", whereby we earn salvation (as some mistakenly do), shows a lack of understanding. The seriousness of the mistake is that this causes one to discount obedience to the plain statements of the Word of God and disregard its instruction, thereby endangering one's soul (Lk. 16:29,31). (A word used to describe this teaching is "Antinomianism").

Biblically, "grace", "faith", "the work of the Spirit", and "obedience" are inextricably intertwined. "Grace" is the source of all, but its idea is incomplete without the others. Paul declares that we have "received *grace*... for *obedience* to the *faith*..." (Rom. 1:5). God's commandments are "made known to all nations for the *obedience* of *faith*" (Rom. 16:26). In Acts 6:7, priests are recorded as having been *obedient* to the *faith*.

*"And by **faith** Abraham **obeyed** (Heb. 11:8).*

We are elect through sanctification of the *Spirit* unto *obedience* (I Peter 1:2). Also, we are they who have "purified your souls in *obeying* the truth through the *Spirit*" (I Pet. 1:22) - and so forth.

Our ethical behavior is to correspond to what God has enabled us to be by adoption and grace based on God's historical, once-for-all act in Christ's death and resurrection. Any other conduct denies the grounding of the believer's new life. Ethics is not an appendage to grace, and ethical admonitions are not one of several ways in which theology can be applied.[30] Thus, for one to teach or act contrary to the scripture and attempt to justify it by claiming that obedience is "works" or "legalism" (or some such) is simply false doctrine, and to follow such is folly.

Love The Reason

In the purest sense of christianity, the believer should not do things on any other basis than love for (and a sense of allegiance to) Jesus Christ. There are practical reasons for maintaining standards in one's life. These may include such things as a sense of responsibility to set an example for one's children, to maintain domestic peace, to avoid upsetting one's parents or other loved ones. To do things for these reasons is not wrong; and very well may be the wisest thing one should do to have a better life and give others happiness. Even on these grounds, I would encourage one to follow truth and do what is best for the whole of a situation, and not to do selfishly to the hurt of others.

Another reason we should or should not do something is the fact of others who seek to impose their will upon us. Sometimes this is proper, while at other times it is not. For example, a parent has an obligation to train their offspring in the ways of the Lord, and should therefore teach them basic ethical and life-style guidelines. By making certain things obligatory, the child is given a framework from which to later work out a personal ethic which is acceptable to themselves, society, and (if they are a christian) to God. Ideally, the parents convey correct perspectives, and the child eventually incorporates them as his/her own.

A local community of believers, to be a "community", also holds an agreed upon set of values. Hopefully, these values accurately reflect the teachings and spirit of the Word of God. Thus to the extent a local church develops, articulates, and embraces these values, it is bonded in a spiritual commonality with the Word and with one another. A local church (under the leadership of a God-anointed pastor) has as part of its mission the responsibility to expose to the world the truth of God. This is done in numerous ways, including teaching, spirit, life-style, etc. Some standards will reflect not only the concerns of the local church body, as each individual is the temple of God, but will also reflect valid concerns of the broader society at large. These will be (and should be) espoused in the civil arena through the political, social, and civic institutions set up for governance of such. However, there are other "personal" life-style standards which are important to those who are the present-day temple of God by virtue of the infilling of the Holy Spirit and bearing the name of Christ. These are not standards which the church body should attempt to superimpose upon everybody - for the simple reason that they are significant only because of the distinct fact (and honor) that God's people are exclusively the present personal dwelling place of God on earth at this time.

Not only does the local church body hold common sets of beliefs, values, and ethical standards, but this is also true of larger communities such as church organizations and religious movements. The very fact that there are many such groups is generally due to emphasis on particular scriptural truths which they (or someone they have followed) discovered and espoused. Thus, if a large constellation of churches hold as dear particular doctrines and ethical truths that God has given them, they are certainly responsible for the stewardship of those doctrines and should protect them (I Cor. 4:1). A people simply cannot cohere on the basis of geographical proximity alone. For a people to bond, especially religiously, they must hold a common set of beliefs and have a common cause. From this comes a common fellowship and bonding. If the commonality of beliefs and cause is removed, the bond of fellowship will eventually disintegrate. For fellowship is a result of other factors, and can never maintain itself without basing itself on something else. In christianity in particular, there is a common spiritual life within that makes the whole a "body" with one head (i.e., Christ).

There is much to say on the above, but suffice it here to say that we can see how there are numerous constraining factors which become forces in the development and maintenance of one's christian life-style. The power of sociological, familial, and fraternal forces is considerable. Not only are they considerable, but they can be (and often are) brought to bear on a situation in a desperate attempt to prevent someone from departing from basic biblical life-styles. This desperation often reaches such a level that every possible instrument is brought to bear on the situation. Threats, fear, guilt, intimidation, etc., are often brought into play. At least in some instances, there are probably specific times and situations where the use of such things can be temporarily appropriate. The family wants to protect its dignity, so it pressures one to conform. Or the future of the children is called to attention as a familial attempt to continue one's conformity. On the local church level, many of the same kind of tactics are sometimes used. Eventually, fear, threats, and intimidation are marshalled to maintain control and conformity. Sometimes, when the battle wages hot enough, any available method is used to get the desired result of containment - oftentimes to the extent that the method used to maintain containment is as onerous as the departure from the standard in question. Fights result, and sometimes both parties end up with exactly the same spirit, even though on different sides of an issue.

Sadly, the same things happen in larger religious groups.

However, in all of this, there is one thing I know - and know unquestionably. Unless your reason for living a biblical lifestyle is because you love Jesus Christ and have a personal covenant love relationship with Him, then your reason is not good enough. One's understanding that being the temple of God sets them unequivocally apart from and above all other considerations, is a necessary revelation. The first question regarding the motivation and obligation of the believer is not "what ought I to do?", but "what has God done for me? What am I, as a believer in Jesus Christ, as the temple of God, and as a member of His church, to do?". The answer is, "I am to do what I am".[31] The authority which God's commands have over us, our understanding of their meaning, and even the ability to carry them out, all stem from the reality that it is our salvation in Christ which now defines our basic identity. These dimensions of God's demand are actualized as (in faith, gratitude, loyalty, and love) we "are ourselves" - our newly created selves.[32]

One will never know what one really is until all else is stripped away, and only this one, lonely, raw, elemental, reason of love is left standing. Some people, and perhaps whole generations, never find out what they are. Their whole life is lived without thought as to "why" they do something. They are seemingly never positioned where the crisis of spiritual self-discovery happens in their lives. That is not true of this generation. This generation has "hit the wall", and all the psychological game playing by those who are apart of it (and/or by its elders) cannot change that. They will know. They will discover what is real. Some will make fatal mistakes from which they will never recover. Others will pursue God relentlessly until the "baby-fat" of hot-house upbringing is driven out of them, and replaced by sober, solid, confident, revelational spiritual strength and muscle. Sadly, it will be seen that some didn't really have "it" in their hearts. Paul writes to those delivered from sin, saying, "...but ye have *obeyed from the heart that form of doctrine which was delivered you*" (Rom. 6:17). Those who have believed "from the head", "from daddy's head", or "from the pastor's head", will be thrown into fretful frustration and confusion. It has always been so. God will have no less. In truth, He is the most demanding general who ever marshalled an army. Only "heart-obedience" is acceptable - heart-submission, heart-devotion, heart-allegiance, heart-passion, nothing else. Anything less is wood, hay, and stubble. It will burn in the purifying fire. Family reasons, community reasons, social reasons, cultural reasons, traditional reasons - all have a place and all have degrees of merit, but none of them qualify to stand in the temple of the sacred and the holy. For it is here where the whole world and all it contains is fallen away, and where heavens angels fall into mute silence. It is here where the glory of God shines with brilliance indescribable, and a Shekinah-stream blasts forth into the furthest reaches of the outer universe. It is here that you will stand alone, with absolutely nothing else in your hand. There will be nothing else. No smiling, compromising preacher who makes a joke out of everything and to whom nothing is reverent. No jeering defender of worldliness. No mocking friends for reinforcement. No scoffing relative in whom to find solace. No supporters in trivializing scripture. Just you. Just you, and your stark, stripped, naked reason. No "material blessing" reasons. No "prosperity now" reasons. No "you gave me joy" reasons. No "I never got sick" reasons. Just one reason. Love! *Love*! *LOVE*! (Yea, it seems I hear the echo of a long- gone God-lover saying: "Though He slay me yet will I trust Him!").

Conclusion

Unfortunately, conscientious christian living can easily degenerate into a form of self-centeredness. Of course, self-centeredness is actually from the "flesh", and not from God at all. Thus, this self-centeredness is no different in fact from the world's self-centeredness, although it may be different in form. When one considers that christianity deals with the most ultimate of things (such as our eternal destiny), it is no wonder that it plumbs the depth of human awareness. In addition, its promise of help to "become", coupled with its claims on one's life as being the dwelling place of God creates further consciousness of one's self. If one is not careful, an abnormal sense of being a wonderful christian can result from occupation with self.

The truth is, when we speak of life-style and ethics, the application of these things far transcends what we have discussed in the preceding pages. These are quite basic. They should be foundational.

Upon them should be built a life of involvement. The christian should plunge into life with a joyful commitment and with the fruit of the Spirit bursting forth out of them in every situation. Our spirituality should result in an awareness of the needy, the downtrodden, and the spiritually deprived. A deep and solidly healthy spirituality will bring us to a life which literally becomes, in its actions, an intercession for the world and its many needs. How we carry out God's mission in each of us will depend upon His personal will for each of us, and the gifts He has imbued each of us with. However, the fact of our involvement shouldn't be a question, but a "given". For God's dwelling place on earth (which we are) was always intended to be a place from which the bounty of God could flow out to the world. It is no different today.

End Notes

1. *The Interpreter's Dictionary Of The Bible*, (Nashville, TN: Abingdon Press, 1962), p. 714

2. Ibid.

3. *The Complete Biblical Library*, Mt. 26:28, (Springfield, MO: 1989), p. 579

4. James Lee Beall, *Rise To Newness Of Life*, (Detroit, MI: Evangel Press, 1974), p. 10

5. Ibid., p. 11

6. *The Complete Biblical Library*, (Springfield, MO: 1991), reference #5262

7. Jay Dwight Pentecost, *The Glory Of God*, (Multnomah Press, 1980), p. 51

8.   *The Interpreter's Dictionary Of The Bible*, vol. 4, p. 317

9.   Jay Dwight Pentecost, *The Glory Of God*, p. 49

10.   For a more indepth study of this subject, see author's book, *The Two Men Of Human History - Adam & Christ*

11.   Jay Dwight Pentecost, *The Glory Of God*, p. 65

12.   Ibid.

13.   Gregory Pope, *No Greater Burden*, (1985), p. 38

14.   *The Complete Biblical Library*, Notes On "Kosmos", I Pet. 3:3

15.   David Wasmundt, *Neo-Phariseeism (sic)*, (Chapel Hill, NC: Professional Press, 1992), p. 148

16.   David Bernard, *Practical Holiness*, (Hazelwood, MO: Word Aflame Press, 1985), p. 186

17.   James Hastings, *The Greater Men And Women Of The Bible*, (Edinburgh, England: T & T Clark, 1946), p. 349

18.   Ibid., pp. 345-347

19. Eerdmans Keil-Delitzsch, *Commentary On The Old Testament* (Grand Rapids, MI: 1986), p. 230

20. James Hastings, *The Greater Men And Women Of The Bible*, p. 335

21. Brown, Driver, Briggs, *The Hebrew And English Lexicon Of The Old Testament*, (London, England: Oxford University Press, 1962), pp. 149, 150

22. Eerdmans Keil-Delitzsch, *Commentary On The Old Testament*, p. 409

23. H.D.M. Spencer, Joseph S. Exell, *Pulpit Commentary*, (McLean, VI: McDonald Publishing Company), p. 355

24. *Preacher's Homiletic Commentary*, p. 288

25. *Crudens Complete Concordance* (Grand Rapids, MI: Zondervan Publishing House, 1949).

26. *Preacher's Homiletic Commentary*

27. David Bernard, *Practical Holiness*, p. 167

28. Barth, Karl, Clark, Edinburgh, *Church Dogmatics*, (1957), p. 565

29. Stephen C. Mott, *Biblical Ethics and Social Change*, (New York: Oxford University Press, 1982), p. 23

30.   Ibid., pp. 24, 26

31.   Versus Berkhof, *Christ And The Powers*, p.
        59, as quoted by Stephen C. Mott in
        Biblical Ethics And Social Change.

32.   Ibid., p. 26